Pearl of Grace

A Path to Find Your Voice and Inner Worth

Grace C.W. Liu

GRACE**SOUL**LUTIONS

Pearl of Grace: A Path to Find Your Voice and Inner Worth
Copyright © 2025 Grace C.W. Liu
First Edition Published by Grace C.W. Liu, GraceSOULutions

Cover Design by I Love My Cover Designs
Edited and Proofread by Sarah Newton-John

ISBN (paperback): 978-1-965652-37-4

Printed in the United States of America.

www.gracesoulutions.com

Get the *Grace in Action Workbook*

As you embark on the *Pearl of Grace* journey, I have created the *Grace in Action Workbook* as a perfect companion guide to help you go deeper on each chapter and begin to walk out the principles in your own life.

Go to gracesoulutions.com/workbook to get your copy.

Dear Reader

Welcome to *Pearl of Grace*, a transformative journey designed to help introverted, covertly shy, and quiet women tap into their inner wisdom, embrace their worth, and speak their truth with confidence and grace.

This isn't about turning you into someone loud or pushy (unless you want to be—then go for it!). It's about uncovering the powerhouse communicator you already are. Think of it as a journey of self-discovery, self-love, and bold, beautiful expression—with a bit of extra sparkle, sass, and a whole lot of YOU.

To support you wherever you are on your journey, I've created two soulful resources to help you take the next step:

- **Know Your Unique Communication Style Quiz**
  Discover how you naturally express yourself so you can speak with more clarity, confidence, and connection. Understanding your communication style helps you unlock deeper relationships and advocate for yourself with more ease.
  - Take the quiz at www.GraceSOULutions.com/quiz

- **Dare to Ask for More—With Grace, Not Guilt: 10 Tips to Ask for What You Want Without Guilt, Fear, or Overthinking (Free Guide)**

  If you've ever stayed silent to avoid conflict, rejection, or being seen as too much, you're not alone. This free guide offers 10 gentle yet powerful tips to help you ask for what you want with confidence, clarity, and grace. Learn how to speak up without guilt, stop overthinking your needs, and honor your voice without apology.
  - Download your free guide at:
    www.GraceSOULutions.com/daretoask

You deserve to be seen, heard, and fully expressed. Let these resources support you as you begin or deepen your *Pearl of Grace* journey.

Whether you start with self-awareness or self-expression, both tools are designed to meet you where you are—and gently guide you toward the voice and power that's always been within you.

With grace and empowerment,

Grace C.W. Liu

The Woman's Truth Awakener & Professional Communication Strategist

Dedication

To the covertly shy and quiet women who dream of speaking their truth and being heard—this book is for you. May it inspire you to embrace your voice, own your worth, and share your unique wisdom with the world.

To my husband, Norman, for your unwavering support, and to my parents, for instilling in me the values that shape who I am today.

This book is for the women who have long been seen as quiet—not because it is their nature, but because they were taught to be. May you break through the ceilings that once confined you, step into your power, and soar.

In your personal life, career, or as an entrepreneur, may you find the courage to speak your truth and create the impact you were always meant to make.

Foreword

It is a profound honor and privilege to write the foreword for *Pearl of Grace*, a book that speaks directly to the hearts of those who have ever felt unseen, unheard, or unworthy.

Grace and I share a journey—one of reclaiming our voice, our power, and our right to be seen and heard. We both emerged from the shadows of cultures that often dictated our worth and induced our silence, but we chose to rise. And now, with this book, Grace has provided a path for others to do the same.

I met Grace through a serendipitous introduction facilitated by Sabrina Victoria in a Zoom networking group. Our connection was immediate, deeply rooted in our shared experiences as Asian women who, for too long, had been conditioned to suppress our voices. Though our paths to self-discovery and empowerment were different, they were also strikingly similar. I had chronicled my own transformation in *I Did Not Miss the Boat – Memoir of a Vietnam Hoa Refugee*, and when I invited Grace to share her story on my livestream podcast *From Surviving to Thriving*, it was evident that her journey was one the world needed to hear.

We both started as timid women, weighed down by cultural expectations, burdened by self-doubt, and hesitant to claim our space in the world. But we refused to stay confined. We fought to break the mold, to challenge the narratives imposed upon us, and to step into our power as speakers, communication coaches, and leaders.

My own journey took a pivotal turn when I brought my story to the TEDxEustis stage in 2019. That experience became the moment people began asking to hear the rest of my story, and it was in the quiet solitude of the COVID-19 lockdown that my memoir was born. It was during this time of reflection and writing that I truly understood the power of sharing one's voice.

This book is an extension of that mission—not only to speak up, but to inspire others so they too can find strength in their voice and use it with confidence and grace.

Pearl of Grace is more than a book; it is a movement, a call to action, and a beacon of hope for introverted, shy, and quiet women who have struggled to articulate their truth. Through the *Pearl of Grace*, Grace provides a transformative framework, guiding readers through Presence, Emotion, Awareness, Resilience, and Learning to Repair. She draws from personal experience, ancient wisdom, and modern communication strategies to help readers unearth their inner power and share it with the world.

The metaphor of the pearl is a powerful one. A pearl does not start as something beautiful; it begins as an irritation, an intrusion, a challenge. Over time, through persistence and the grace of nature, it transforms into something rare, precious, and luminous. This is the journey of every woman who has ever felt small, inadequate, or afraid.

Within each of us, there is a pearl waiting to be discovered—our truth, our worth, our brilliance. But to reveal it, we must have the courage to look within, to embrace our struggles, and to polish away the layers of doubt that obscure our light.

One of the most profound aspects of this book is how it acknowledges the silent battles many women fight. So many of us have been conditioned to believe that our opinions are secondary, that our needs are less important, and that speaking up invites conflict or rejection. This book dismantles those false beliefs. Grace has crafted a path that is gentle yet powerful, providing tools for self-awareness, emotional intelligence, and communication mastery. It teaches us that we do not need to be loud to be heard—we need to be authentic.

We need to trust in the wisdom of our own voice and allow it to flow with clarity, confidence, and grace.

As I reflect on my friendship with Grace, I am reminded of how truly precious it is when two souls connect over a shared understanding of struggle and triumph. What began as a simple introduction has blossomed into a sisterhood—a bond fortified by our commitment to empower others. And this is what *Pearl of Grace* offers to every reader: not just knowledge, but companionship on the journey to self-discovery and self-expression. It is a reminder that we are not alone, that our struggles can be understood by others, and that within each of us lies a pearl waiting to shine.

To those reading this book, know this: Your voice matters. Your story is valuable. You do not need permission to take up space. Within you, there is an ocean of wisdom, love, and power waiting to flow. The journey will not always be easy—there will be moments of doubt, discomfort, and resistance. But keep going. Keep peeling back the layers, keep refining your pearl, and keep stepping into your grace.

Thank you, Grace, for writing this book. Thank you for your courage, your wisdom, and your unwavering dedication to helping women everywhere find their voice. *Pearl of Grace* will be a transformative guide for so many, and I am grateful to witness the impact it will have.

To every reader embarking on this journey—welcome. Your pearl is waiting. Let it shine.

Lea Tran
Author, Speaker, Story Coach, TEDx Coach
Advocate for Living Benefits

A Note Before You Begin

Before we dive into *Pearl of Grace*, I want you to know that this book is more than something you read—it's something you'll experience.

Each chapter offers insights, reflections, and mindset shifts to help you find your voice and speak with confidence and grace. You'll discover personal stories, empowering lessons, and gentle challenges that invite you to release old patterns and build new communication habits.

Throughout this book, you'll find Grace Notes for reflection. These gentle prompts are here to support your journey through the *Pearl of Grace* framework. Use them as invitations to pause, process, and reconnect with your inner wisdom in a way that feels natural to you.

You'll also find Soul Notes to anchor your truth. These deeper reflection questions are designed to help you internalize what you've learned and carry it into your everyday conversations, relationships, and personal growth.

As you read, you'll notice I often refer to both communication and conversation. While the two are related, they're not quite the same. Communication includes the full spectrum of how you express yourself: your words, tone, body language, energy, and even your silence. Conversation, on the other hand, is the back-and-forth exchange that happens between people. You can communicate without saying a word, and you can be in a conversation without truly communicating. Understanding the difference matters, especially for those of us who have been taught to stay quiet, minimize our voice, or feel pressure to speak a certain way.

This book will help you navigate both: how to tune into your full energetic expression and how to engage in meaningful, mutual exchange.

If you'd like to go deeper, I've created two companion tools to support your journey:

- **Grace in Action Workbook**
  A practical workbook with expanded journaling prompts, reflection exercises, and communication practices to help you integrate the *Pearl of Grace* framework into your daily life. Whether you love writing things out, need time to process, or want to apply these lessons in real time, the workbook was created with you in mind.

- **Grace Notes Card Deck**
  A 63-card reflection deck offering soulful prompts, gentle mindset shifts, and communication cues. Use it daily or intuitively, either as a companion to this book or on its own, to support grounding, clarity, and authentic expression.

Start when you are ready. There is no "right" way to do this. Only your way—and that is more than enough.

Throughout this book, I'll be referring to covertly shy and quiet women. So, let's clear up what I mean by this: Covertly shy women hesitate in social interactions because self-doubt has them second-guessing everything. Covertly quiet women have thoughts, opinions, and ideas but keep them locked inside, even when they want to share.

Maybe you see yourself in one category. Maybe you see yourself in both. Either way, you are exactly where you need to be.

Table of Contents

Introduction:
The Pearl of Grace™

Growing up in a traditional Chinese household, I learned early on that staying quiet was often easier than speaking up. I wasn't shy about meeting new people, but voicing my own thoughts, especially when they clashed with others, was a very different story. Rocking the boat wasn't just discouraged—it was downright dangerous. My parents, rooted in their Eastern upbringing, saw obedience as a virtue, and every time I dared to challenge their views, I was met with swift, unwavering authority. Over time, I got the message: My voice didn't matter.

But silence has a price. The more I swallowed my words, the smaller I felt. The smaller I felt, the less worthy I believed myself to be.

A defining moment came at my high school graduation; what should have been a celebration turned into a wound that cut deep.

I had finally been allowed to wear makeup for the first time (a monumental occasion in itself). While I stood in front of the mirror, carefully applying each layer with excitement, my mom approached me. Instead of pride, she expressed disappointment and shame that I hadn't graduated with honors like my cousins.

1

In traditional Chinese and Asian families, academic achievement—especially graduating with honors—is seen as a vital marker of success. It mattered deeply to my parents and extended family. But for me, simply graduating and being accepted into university felt like a huge accomplishment. I was proud. I was ready. But in her eyes, I had failed.

And then came the gut punch. "**I should have listened to your grandmother and had you aborted.**"

That moment something shattered inside me.

Walking across that stage to receive my diploma felt hollow. People congratulated me, but I could barely respond. Not because I wasn't grateful, but because I felt undeserving. The shame cast upon me swallowed any joy I might have felt. And in that moment, I learned a brutal truth:

"Sticks and stones may break my bones, but words will never hurt me," is a damn lie.

Words do hurt. They cut. They shape us in ways we don't even realize until years later when we're still picking up the broken pieces.

For years, I carried the weight of my mother's words, internalizing them as proof of my inadequacy. But life has a way of handing us wake-up calls, and mine came years later in the form of an argument with my husband. Frustration boiled over, and before I knew it, I hurled cruel words at him—words that carried the same sting I had once endured. And then, he did something that stopped me cold. He ran and hit his head against the wall, overwhelmed by the pain of my words.

It was a gut-wrenching moment of realization. The very patterns I had suffered from, I was now repeating. My inability to express myself with clarity and grace wasn't just hurting me, it was hurting the people I loved. That moment jolted me awake. It became my turning point.

I had to break the cycle. I dove deep into self-discovery, devouring books, enrolling in programs, and exploring every tool I could find such as Myers-Briggs, Enneagram, Human Design, EFT (Emotional Freedom Tapping), Reiki, mindfulness, journaling, Quantum Level Reprogramming. I was determined to heal, not just for myself but for my relationships, and for my future.

And in the process, I found something extraordinary—my **pearl**.

A pearl doesn't just appear; it forms through irritation, through challenge, through persistence. To me, it became a symbol of wisdom, worthiness, and truth, and the very things I had spent my life suppressing. And through grace I learned self-acceptance, forgiveness, and love. I learned how to polish that pearl and let it shine.

Now, let's be real: This journey wasn't all epiphanies and enlightenment. There were messy moments, hard truths, and plenty of, '*What the hell am I even doing?*' phases. I faced my flaws as well as my strengths, my generosity and flexibility, and yes, also my stubbornness, my quick temper, and my knee-jerk reactions. But the more I embraced every part of me, the less the "ugly" parts took control. Self-acceptance became my superpower.

And that's why I'm here, and that's why this book exists.

Because I know I'm not alone in this.

What I've seen in myself and in the covertly shy, quiet women I've worked with is that many of us have been taught, consciously or subconsciously, to stay small. Maybe someone told us to be "seen, not heard." Maybe we were ridiculed for speaking up. Maybe one painful moment made us shut down completely. Whatever the reason, we learned to shrink, to silence ourselves, to hide.

But here's the thing: We're not naturally timid, shy, or quiet. Deep down, there's a part of us screaming to be seen and heard. We don't want to disappear. We want to *shine*. We want to say to the world, **"Here I am. Hear me roar. I am a big deal!"**

But because of past experiences, traumas, or outdated beliefs, we've convinced ourselves it's safer to stay in the shadows. We've mistaken silence for safety.

But the pearl inside us? It doesn't want to stay hidden. It's waiting for us to rise up, step into our grace, and finally let our brilliance shine.

This book, *Pearl of Grace*, is my invitation to you: to find your pearl, to embrace your worth, and to walk the path of grace. Each chapter will guide you through this journey, using the acronyms PEARL and GRACE to illuminate the way. You'll find stories, exercises, and reflections to help you discover your inner wisdom, express yourself authentically, and communicate with confidence.

Because here's the thing: Communication isn't just about words. It's about energy. It's about showing up, being seen, being heard, and being understood—not just by others, but by yourself, too.

I share my story not to dwell on the past, but to show you that **transformation is possible**.

If you've ever felt silenced, unworthy, or unsure of how to express your truth, this book is for you.

Your journey starts here, with the first step: **Presence and Perceive Your Truth**. That painful experience at my graduation taught me an invaluable lesson: that feeling worthy is the foundation of speaking your truth. Trust me when I say this- **you are so damn worthy**.

Let's begin.

Part 1

The PEARL Within

Five Keys to Own Your Voice, Be Heard, Be Bold, Be You

Why *Pearl of Grace*? Each letter in PEARL represents a powerful step in your journey that will guide you to break free from silence, fear, and self-doubt so you can shine in your own right. Time to stop being invisible. Let's get you stepping into the spotlight where you belong.

A pearl doesn't start out as a flawless gem; it forms through layers of resilience. Just like the oyster transforms an irritant into something beautiful, your past experiences, even the tough ones have shaped you into the powerful, wise woman you are today.

For many introverted, covertly shy, and quiet women, life has been about learning to stay silent, playing small, or feeling unworthy. Maybe you were told to keep quiet. Perhaps you were laughed at for speaking up. Over time, you built layers of protection around yourself, believing it was safer to stay hidden. But here's the truth: your voice was never meant to be silenced. Your pearl has always been there, waiting for you to reveal its brilliance.

Just as each layer added to a pearl transforms it into something luminous, each PEARL step transforms a part of your inner world. Presence sets the foundation by helping you reclaim your space and tune in to your energy. Emotions reveal your truth and guide you toward honoring your boundaries without guilt. Awareness clarifies your voice, aligning what you say with what you mean so your message carries power. Resilience strengthens your ability to bounce back and show up with confidence, even after difficult moments.

And Love helps you learn to repair and reconnect, so your words create healing instead of harm.

This journey isn't about "fixing" yourself. It's about peeling back the layers of fear and doubt to reveal the radiant, powerful communicator you've always been. And trust me, the world is ready for you.

P – Presence & Perceive Your Truth

First things first, owning your truth. Through self-awareness and personality frameworks like Human Design, you'll begin to understand how your energy shapes the way you communicate, connect, and express yourself. This section includes reflective exercises and journaling prompts drawn from the YOU MATTER card deck to help you embrace your uniqueness and own your presence. Stop fading into the background because it's time to claim your space like the special and significant human you are.

For deeper exploration with additional tools, including the Enneagram, be sure to check out the companion workbook, *Grace in Action Workbook: A Practical Companion Workbook to Pearl of Grace.* You can also explore the Grace Notes card deck for additional reflection prompts and practices to support your presence and communication with clarity and compassion.

E – Emotions & Embrace Your Worthiness

Ever struggled with knowing when to speak up and when to stay silent? Here, you'll learn how to tune into your emotions and the energy of communication to honor your boundaries. True worthiness isn't just about knowing you deserve respect. It's about standing firm in your energy so others respect and honor your boundaries, too. No more second-guessing yourself or over-explaining. Just pure, unapologetic self-worth, dripping with confidence *like your favorite power outfit.*

A – Awareness & Asserting Your Voice

This step is all about becoming aware of the way you speak to communicate with clarity, confidence, and grace. You'll learn how to align your voice with your message to carry the power you intend, no longer sounding timid when you really mean business! With practical tools for assertive (not aggressive) communication, you'll develop a voice that is strong, clear, and unmistakably *yours.* Think powerful, think magnetic, think YOU, unleashed. Time to drop the mic (figuratively, of course!).

R – Resilience & Radiate Confidence

You've overcome challenges, maybe even traumas, and that resilience has shaped you into the incredible person you are today. Resilience builds the foundation for true confidence. Confidence isn't just about what you say; it's about how you say it. This section focuses on mastering body language, tone of voice, and the energy behind your communication to help you radiate confidence. Now, it's time to let that strength shine. Stop hiding. Your voice deserves center stage. Ready to own it?

L – Love & Learn to Repair

Communication breakdowns happen, but what if you could manage them with grace rather than fear? This final step teaches you how to repair conversations and relationships from a place of love, empathy, and accountability. Put an end to avoiding tough talks or bottling things up. Instead, you'll confidently navigate misunderstandings with ease, ensuring your voice is heard without unnecessary conflict or blame. Your words are powerful. Let's make them count. No messy drama is needed.

If you're navigating past communication wounds or want guided support for practicing repair conversations, you'll find additional prompts and exercises in the companion workbook, *Grace in Action Workbook: A Practical Companion Workbook to Pearl of Grace.*

You can also pull cards from the Grace Notes: A 63-Card Deck for Soulful Reflection, to support your voice with clarity, compassion, and confidence—especially when you need a quick reset, reflection, or realignment before or after a tough conversation.

You were never meant to be small. You were born to speak, shine, and soar—with grace.

Are you ready to shine? If you've ever felt like you were meant to speak up, share your story, and make an impact but weren't sure how, then this path is for you. You don't have to roar to be heard (unless you want to, of course!). What you need to do is embrace your own voice, your own power, and your own unique way of expressing yourself.

Your journey begins now. Let's uncover your pearl, step into your grace, and make sure the world hears what you have to say. Are you in?

Let's do this!

Chapter 1

Own Your Presence, Own Your Truth

Listen Up, Beautiful Soul—It Starts with You

Before you even think about speaking up, know that your voice is powerful, but only if you know how to wield it. Confident communication starts with listening not to others, but to yourself.

That means tuning in to your inner wisdom, the voice inside that's been dying to be heard. Before you can truly own your words, you need to own who you are. It's time to peel back the layers of fear, doubt, and hesitation that have been holding you back, a bit like a bad Wi-Fi signal.

This journey isn't about simply "learning to speak up", it's about stepping into your presence with conviction. It's about finally occupying the space you were always meant to. When you do that, your communication naturally shifts from passive to powerful, from overlooked to unforgettable, from fearful to fierce. Because, who wants to live life on mute?

Staying present isn't always easy. In a world that pulls your attention in a hundred different directions at once, presence takes *practice*; it takes intention. The reality is that most of us are barely holding eye contact with the moment we're actually in.

Distraction is the norm these days. We live in a world where multitasking is practically a badge of honor. But here's the problem: You're texting while having a conversation, and now you have no clue what was just said. You're nodding at someone while mentally drafting your grocery list. You're half-listening, because your brain is busy replaying that one embarrassing thing you did five years ago.

Sound familiar? We've all been there. Communication is more than words, it's an energy exchange. And if your energy is split between 50 different places, you aren't really communicating—you're just making noise.

Think of presence like a personal power source. When you're fully plugged in, your communication is magnetic. People feel your energy before you say a single word. As you cultivate presence, you command attention without needing to raise your voice. You create deeper connections by being fully engaged. People feel heard, valued, and understood. You reduce misunderstandings because you're tuned in. You're present.

When you bring grounded, focused energy into a conversation, it creates a safe space for others to be real with you. People open up when they feel heard. They trust you when they sense your sincerity. And when you're fully present, your words carry weight and your voice becomes unforgettable.

Before we dive deeper, I want you to know that everything I'm about to share isn't just theory—it's been lived. I didn't wake up one day magically confident and present. I struggled, got lost in self-doubt, and had to learn how to come home to myself. I'm sharing my story because I want you to see that this path is possible. After that, I'll walk you through exactly how you can begin to anchor your own presence, step by step.

Let me take you back to that day that should have been filled with celebration and pride—my high school graduation. Instead of basking in the joy of the moment, I was hit with a revelation that shook me to my core.

For years, I believed that when my mom found out she was pregnant with me, abortion was never even considered. My dad always shared the story that he had only $50 to his name at the time my mom was pregnant, and that everyone in the family welcomed me wholeheartedly when I was born.

But on the very day I was supposed to be celebrating one of the biggest milestones of my life, I found out that wasn't quite true. They had considered not having me at all.

And just like that, graduation became a battlefield of emotions rather than a joyful milestone. In place of feeling loved, accomplished, and celebrated, I felt like a mistake, and that my existence had been a burden instead of a blessing. The weight of that realization crushed me, and an argument with my mother that day cemented those wounds deep into my soul.

That moment was a wake-up call, but not in the way you might think. Rather than moving forward, I buried myself in self-doubt, guilt, and fear. My inner dialogue became a relentless loop of: *'Am I even supposed to be here? Was I ever truly wanted? Do I even matter?'*

I spent years living in that mental prison, constantly replaying past pain or worrying about what others thought of me. I wasn't living, I was just existing—stuck in the past, paralyzed by a future I feared. I became an expert at making myself small, invisible, and muted because somewhere deep inside, I believed that maybe that's what I was meant to be.

Life has a way of nudging (or sometimes shoving) us toward the truth. I hit a point where I couldn't keep living in my head anymore. I had wasted so much energy on things I couldn't change, and I was exhausted.

I made a decision. I decided to show up for myself. I decided to be present in my own life. I decided that my voice and my presence deserved space in this world. And let me tell you that this shift wasn't easy. It didn't happen overnight. Some days, it was like wading through emotional quicksand. But with every step, I felt lighter, stronger, and more free.

I learned how to anchor myself in the present as an alternative to drowning in old wounds or fears of the future. I learned how to listen to myself without judgment or fear. And the most beautiful part?

I found my voice. No longer did I shrink myself down to fit into spaces that didn't honor me. I stopped overthinking and started speaking from a place of truth, power, and presence.

If I could do it? *So can you.*

Being physically present isn't the same as being truly present. You can sit in a room with someone and be miles away in your head. You can nod along in a conversation while mentally planning dinner. Let's be honest, how often do you check your phone, mid-conversation?

If you want to own your presence, command attention, and feel fully grounded in your conversations, you need to train your brain to stop wandering, to anchor yourself and become grounded. This isn't just some "woo-woo" concept—it's actually a game-changer.

Here are several ways you can anchor yourself in the moment so you can show up as the fully engaged, confident powerhouse you're meant to be. These small but mighty shifts aren't just tips, I've used them myself. Every tool and suggestion in this book is something I've personally practiced. I don't just talk the talk—I walk it, too. And as you move through these pages, you'll find yourself returning to these strategies again and again to strengthen your presence and own your voice with conviction.

Mindful Breathing: The Instant Reset Button

Have you ever felt your mind racing a million miles a minute? This is your cue to breathe. Not that shallow, distracted kind of breathing, but the intentional, deep breathing that brings you back to the present.

Try this:
Inhale deeply through your nose (like you're smelling a rose).
Hold for a moment (count to four).
Exhale slowly through your mouth (like you're blowing out a candle).
Repeat until you feel centered.
Breathing like this is a lifesaver before nerve-wracking conversations, presentations, or anytime your energy starts to scatter.

Grounding Techniques: Feel the Earth Beneath You

When you feel overwhelmed, scattered, or just "off," ground yourself. Grounding helps you come back to your body, back to the moment, and back to your power. It's not *woo*—it's wisdom. The fastest way to stop spiraling in your head is to reconnect with the earth beneath your feet.

17

Stand up tall and firm.

Plant your feet firmly on the ground. Soften your knees, drop your shoulders.

Imagine roots growing from your feet into the earth, pulling up strength, stability, and presence.

Take a slow, deep breath in through your nose (smell the rose) and slowly breathe out through your mouth (blow out the candle)

This is your power stance. When you ground yourself like this, your voice, body language, and energy shift instantly and people can feel when you're rooted in your power.

Active Listening: Be All-In or Don't Bother

Most people "listen" while thinking about what they're going to say next. Not you. Being truly present means listening to *understand*, not just to respond.

Next time you're in a conversation, challenge yourself:

No interrupting.

No formulating your response while they're still talking.

No checking out mentally.

Instead, just listen. Nod, absorb, and give your full attention.

People notice when you do this, and it builds trust, connection, and influence faster than anything else.

Self-Reflection: Know Thyself, Own Thyself

You can't communicate confidently if you don't know who you are or what you stand for. One of my favorite tools for this? My "YOU MATTER, YES YOU DO" card deck and journal. Reflection and journaling helps you uncover insights you'd otherwise ignore.

Take time to meditate, reflect and journal on:

18

Your thoughts
Your emotions
Your triggers and reactions
Your patterns in communication

Digital Detox: Unplug to Plug Back Into Life

Your presence is competing with notifications, scrolling, and the constant noise of the digital world. How many times a day do you check your phone? If you want to be more present, set some boundaries.

- Designate "no-phone zones" (like during meals or deep conversations).
- Mute unnecessary notifications (your email can wait).
- Take social media breaks because even a few hours can make a difference.

Unplug and watch how much richer your connections become.

Daily Presence Practice: Make It a Ritual

Presence isn't a one-time thing, it's a muscle. The more you train it, the stronger it gets. The more you consciously practice being present, the more natural it becomes.

- Start your morning with a 5-minute grounding exercise or meditation.
- Take mindful walks, paying attention to your surroundings instead of rushing.
- End your day by reflecting on when you felt present and when you checked out.

Being present is about more than merely showing up, it's about showing up fully. Being present means paying attention. And when you do, magic happens. Being present is about cutting through the mental clutter and aligning yourself—mind, body, and spirit, so that when you do speak, your words land with clarity and impact.

Have you ever heard of EQ?

EQ is your emotional intelligence; it's your superpower. Presence and EQ go hand in hand. The more in tune you are with your emotions (and the emotions of those around you), the more powerful and effective your communication becomes. Later on we'll dive deeper into your emotional truth and emotional regulation and the role they play in the *Pearl of Grace*.

Presence is the spark that supercharges your emotional intelligence. When you start leading with EQ, it shows up in powerful ways—like these:

Self-Awareness – You recognize when emotions are creeping in and adjust accordingly.
Self-Regulation – Rather than reacting impulsively, you pause, process, and respond with intention.
Social Awareness – You pick up on unspoken cues, energy shifts, and emotional undercurrents in a room.
Relationship Management – You use all of the above to navigate conversations with grace, clarity, and impact.

People with high EQ don't just communicate, they connect. And connection? That's where the magic happens. Because being present isn't just about stillness. It's about *sensing*. Feeling. Attuning. And that makes your words land with depth and truth. No debate. No need to prove it. *YOU MATTER!*

Presence means knowing your worth, honoring your needs, and understanding that self-care is not a luxury, it's a necessity. And yet, how many times have you put yourself on the back burner? How often have you run yourself ragged trying to be everything for everyone else while barely keeping yourself afloat?

Enough of that.

If you don't take care of yourself, you *cannot* take care of others. Period.

Imagine your body is a car. When your tank is full, you're cruising, handling life, knocking out tasks, and maybe even helping a friend by driving her across town for an appointment. You've got the capacity to do it all.

What happens when you're down to a quarter tank? You've got just enough gas to handle your own errands, but not enough to go out of your way to pick someone else up. You have a choice. You can push through, run on fumes, and risk breaking down. Or, be honest, prioritize your needs, and let your friend figure out another way.

Here's where the guilt creeps in. That voice in your head says, "But I should help. I should figure it out. I should just push through." *No.* You should take care of yourself first. If you don't, then what? You burn out. You break down. You start resenting the very people you want to support. And when your energy is drained, how much can you really give? Not much.

When you're running on full energy, you can give freely. You feel good about helping others because you're already taken care of. But when you're running on empty, every favor feels like another weight dragging you down.

Here's the real talk: ***you are not responsible for solving everyone's problems.*** Read that again.

21

Presence isn't just about engaging with the world. It's about engaging with yourself. It's knowing when to step up and when to step back. It's recognizing that your needs matter just as much as anyone else's.

If you need permission to prioritize yourself without guilt, consider this: Self-care isn't selfish. Self-care is power. It's sustainability. It's what allows you to show up, be present, and give to others without losing yourself in the process.

That's the kind of presence that changes everything.

Now that you understand how to anchor yourself in the present, how to be truly here, not just physically, but mentally, emotionally, and energetically, it's time to go deeper. Presence is just the beginning. When you're fully present, you create the space to hear yourself clearly: your needs, your values, your desires.

And that's where your truth lives.

Not the watered-down version you've shown the world, but the real, untamed, undeniable truth that's been waiting for you to claim it.

If you haven't gotten your Grace in Action Workbook, now is a great time to pause and get it so you can go deeper on what you've just learned and put the concepts... into action!

Go to gracesoulutions.com/workbook. You're welcome to also grab a journal you have and write your responses to the prompts that follow.

Grace Notes

Mini-Journal Prompts:

1. What parts of your voice have you hidden—and what are you ready to reclaim?

2. Which of the presence practices shared in this chapter resonated with you the most—mindful breathing, grounding, active listening, self-reflection, digital detox, or daily rituals?

3. What perhaps distracted you from being present today—and how can you gently bring yourself back next time?

Soul Notes:

Choose one of the practices above and write about how you'll incorporate it into your daily rhythm this week.

Remember, presence isn't perfection—it's a practice. Every small shift adds up.

Chapter 2

Perceiving Your Inner Truth: Who Are You, Really?

Unlearn the Rules. Peel Back the Layers. Reclaim the Real You.

Now that you're mastering presence, it's time to take your journey a step further. Let's discover more about you and your inner truth. Answer these questions about yourself. Who are you when no one's watching? What energy do you bring into the world? How do you show up in conversations?

Being present is powerful, but self-awareness is what makes that presence magnetic. If you don't understand your own energy, communication style, and strengths, you'll keep second-guessing yourself. And that means, you'll never know WHO YOU ARE.

Most of us have spent so much time filtering, shrinking, and adjusting ourselves to fit the mold that we've forgotten what we even sound like, unfiltered. You weren't born second-guessing yourself. That was taught.

Before the world piled on expectations, before you learned to edit yourself for approval, you were free. You spoke your mind. You laughed loud. You moved through life without overanalyzing every word that came out of your mouth.

Find your truth. The one not shaped by other people's comfort levels. Not the one adjusted to avoid conflict, but the real, unfiltered, fully expressed YOU. It's time to let her out.

If you've ever nodded along to something you didn't agree with to keep the peace, congratulations, you've been trained well. Women, especially quiet and introverted ones, are conditioned from a young age to be agreeable, likable, and non-disruptive.

So, how do you do find your truth? You start by unlearning the rules that were never yours to follow in the first place. You pause and reflect, not on who the world wants you to be, but on who you really are underneath all the layers. It's about reconnecting with your inner truth, the version of you that existed before the world told you to be smaller, quieter, more agreeable.

Here's how you begin:

Get Curious About Yourself
Start asking bold questions without judgment:
- What lights me up?
- What drains me?
- What am I pretending not to know?
- What do I believe that no longer serves me?

Notice The Moment You Shrink

Pay attention to the moments you silence yourself or mold your words to make others more comfortable. These are clues. Each one points to a place where your voice is ready to come forward.

Write it Out, Speak it Out

Give your message a voice, even if it starts as a whisper. Journal. Talk to yourself out loud. Practice saying what you really mean, even if it's messy. Truth doesn't need to be perfect. It just needs to be honest.

Start Small, But Start

You don't have to shout from the rooftops (unless you want to). Start by honoring your truth in everyday moments by saying "No" when you mean no, speak up when something doesn't feel right, and stop apologizing for simply existing.

Surround Yourself With Permission-Givers

Spend time with people who celebrate the real you, not just the polished or filtered version. The more you're around authenticity, the easier it is to live it.

Truth isn't just about the words you speak, it's about what you feel while you speak them. You know that gut feeling when something's off? That moment you know exactly what you want to say, but the words get stuck behind hesitation? That's not an accident. That's conditioning. Years of silencing yourself, second-guessing your instincts, and choosing safety over self-expression leave a lasting imprint. As you're in alignment with your intention, you feel grounded, strong, and certain—even if your voice shakes. Your words come from a deep place inside you, not just the surface. Conversations leave you energized, not drained, because you're showing up fully as yourself.

When you're suppressing your divine expression, it feels heavy like you're carrying the weight of all the things you didn't say. Frustration builds because nobody seems to understand you, and you get stuck replaying conversations, self-editing, and wishing you had spoken up. Truth is a feeling as much as it is a statement.

Here's your new rule: if speaking your inner wisdom feels like freedom, it's right. If staying silent feels like suffocation, it's time to change that inner voice.

If you've spent years quieting your voice, it's time to turn the volume back up, gradually, if you need to, but consistently. This isn't about going from silent to "screaming" overnight. It's about taking small, powerful steps toward owning your voice, your experience, and your space.

Here are some things you can start doing now to reclaim your brilliance. I know they are hard, and it will take practice. Go back to those grounding exercises and what you journaled.

Say no without cushioning it with excuses. No long-winded explanations, no unnecessary guilt. Just "No, that doesn't work for me." Period.

Stop saying "I don't care" when you actually *do*. Pick the restaurant, choose the movie, and have an opinion. You're allowed.

Correct people when they misinterpret you. If someone puts words in your mouth or assumes your stance on something, set the record straight.

Express a boundary and hold it. You're not responsible for how others react to your perspective. You are responsible for honoring it.

Every time you choose to speak up over shrinking down, you reclaim a piece of yourself.

You don't have to be the loudest voice in the room to be powerful. Own your voice without apology. No more watering yourself down to be more digestible. Speak boldly. Speak clearly. Speak like you belong, because you do.

How you talk to yourself matters. More than you think. Are you hyping yourself up like the powerhouse you are, or are you dragging yourself down with doubt and criticism? Are you fueling your confidence, or are you handing the mic over to that nagging inner voice that says, "You're not good enough, so why even try?"

The way you speak to yourself shapes your reality. Think about it. Would you ever talk to a friend the way you sometimes talk to yourself? Would you look them in the eye and say, "You always mess up. You're a failure. You should just quit." Hell no. So why do you say it to yourself?

The truth is, we are constantly creating stories in our minds. And if you keep telling yourself you're not capable, not worthy, or not enough, then guess what? Your mind will *believe* it. And when your mind believes it, you start living like it's true.

But what if you reframed the story? What if, as an alternative to telling yourself you're not good enough, you asked:

- What if I AM more powerful than I realize?
- What if this challenge is just proof that I AM growing?
- What if my so-called "failures" are stepping stones to something bigger?
- What if my current truth isn't the truth—and I can change it?

The Power of Perspective: Seeing Beyond One Truth

Perceiving your truth isn't just about knowing your perspective, it's about realizing that your perspective isn't the only one.

Ever walked away from a conversation feeling dismissed? Maybe you thought, "They don't take me seriously." But pause. Could it be that they were distracted? Stressed? Processing in their own way?

Or maybe you put yourself out there, applied for a job, pitched an idea, shared your feelings, only to be met with rejection. Does that mean you're not good enough? Or could it mean you're simply being redirected toward something that's meant for you?

Your perception shapes your reality. But here's the game-changer: you control your perception.

Your inner dialogue matters. It's that voice in your head that no one hears but you... and it can be either your greatest ally or your harshest enemy. Every time you face a challenge, a setback, or something doesn't go as planned, you have two choices:

Let Self-Doubt Run the Show

You know this voice: "Why did I even try?" "Of course this happened. I'm not good enough." "I should've known better." It's the voice that echoes every criticism you've ever heard, every moment you felt small or silenced. It sounds familiar because it's been rehearsed a thousand times.

Find a New Truth

This is the voice you're still learning to trust. The one that says: "What if this isn't failure, it's feedback?" "What if I'm growing through this?" "What if I'm stronger and wiser because of what I just faced?" This voice isn't delusional, it's empowering. It's the voice that helps you get back up, not because you have something to prove, but because you believe you're worth it.

Remember, your new truth is changing that inner talk. You're talking to yourself as your best friend. You are your biggest cheerleader. Stop being your own worst critic.

Try these reframing practices:

Finish with swallowing words that deserve to be spoken. Stop muting yourself to make others comfortable. The "good girl" act might have protected you in the past, but it's not serving you anymore. It's time to break free.

Your voice isn't a problem that needs fixing. Your opinions aren't too much. Your experience isn't up for debate. It's time to reclaim your power.

If you haven't gotten your Grace in Action Workbook, now is a great time to pause and get it so you can go deeper on what you've just learned and put the concepts... into action!

Go to gracesoulutions.com/workbook. You're welcome to also grab a journal you have and write your responses to the prompts that follow.

Grace Notes

Mini-Journal Prompts:

1. Think about the last time you nodded along, stayed silent and quieted your truth. What was the cost of staying small?

2. When was the last time you said "Yes" to something, and you really meant no. What would it feel like to say "No"?

3. What's one belief about yourself or your voice that you're ready to let go of? How has it held you back, and what new truth would you rather believe instead?

Soul Notes

As if speaking to a beloved friend, rewrite your inner message. Then read it out loud.

You weren't born quiet—you were taught to shrink. This is you, becoming whole again.

Chapter 3

Unlocking Your Voice: The Power of Human Design in Communication

The Energetic Blueprint to Unlocking Your Unique Voice

Not all communication blueprints are created equal. Some of us are natural initiators, while others need to be invited into conversations. Some people thrive on deep discussions, while others prefer to keep it light and to the point.

And guess what? That's not just personality—it's ENERGY.

Enter Human Design, a system that blends astrology, energy centers, and quantum mechanics (yes, really, not as woo-woo as it sounds) to show you how your energy naturally flows in communication. Think of it as your communication DNA. The ultimate cheat code for understanding yourself and others.

When I first learned that I was a Manifesting Generator, it felt like unlocking a level in a video game I didn't even know I was playing. Suddenly, so much clicked. I thrive when I respond to what's already happening around me, not when I force things into motion. I've learned that I'm meant to inform others before I take action, or the energy fizzles out. And when I try to initiate without that spark of response? Frustration hits fast.

Boom. Suddenly, everything made sense.

For years, I LOVED giving advice, but no one ever took it. Why? Because I was initiating when I should have been waiting for the invitation to respond. I'd say something, get ignored, and then five minutes later, someone else would say the exact same thing, and suddenly it was groundbreaking wisdom. I was ready to scream.

But once I leaned into my Human Design and waited for people to ask for my input, things shifted. Not only was my advice heard, but it was appreciated. And it applies to everything—even writing this book.

A friend kept telling me to write a book (over and over again). At first, I brushed it off. But when the message kept coming, I RESPONDED. I told my husband and my community, and suddenly the right people, the right resources, and the right timing aligned perfectly.

That's the magic of knowing your energy and communicating in alignment with it. I used to feel invisible, like my words didn't land until someone else repeated them. It was maddening at the time. But now I see it differently.

It wasn't that what I said lacked value. It was that the timing and the energy weren't aligned. Once I started waiting for the invitation and the right feeling of energy, my voice began to resonate in the right moments, with the right people.

That shift happened when I leaned into my Human Design and allowed others to come to me first. When people asked for my input, my advice wasn't just heard. It was welcomed. That's when I truly understood the power of knowing your energy and communicating in alignment with it.

Your Human Design type influences how you express yourself, make decisions, and connect with others. There are five main types in the Human Design system. To find out yours, you'll need your birth date, time, and place. A list of chart generators is provided in the resource section at the end of this book.

Here's a brief summary of each type to help you get started and understand how your communication is uniquely wired.

1. Manifestors – The Initiators: "I'm going to do this, and you just need to keep up."

- Strengths: Bold, visionary, and trailblazing.

- Communication Tip: You NEED to inform people before taking action, or they'll resist you. (No, they're not trying to control you. They just need a heads-up!)

- Challenge: You might get frustrated when people don't instantly understand or follow your lead.

2. Generators – The Builders: "I'm in my zone when I'm doing what lights me up."

- Strengths: Steady, committed, and magnetic when excited.

- Communication Tip: Wait for something to spark your interest before engaging. If it doesn't excite you, it's a hard "No".

- Challenge: Saying "Yes" too often and burning out (you don't have to respond to everything).

3. Manifesting Generators – The Multitasking Powerhouses: "I can do 10 things at once, and I thrive on momentum!"

- Strengths: Quick learners, multi-passionate, and adaptable.

- Communication Tip: Respond first, then inform others about what you're doing. (Otherwise, people think you're all over the place!)

- Challenge: Slowing down enough to explain your process so others can follow.

4. Projectors – The Guides: "I see things differently. Let me help you work smarter, not harder."

- Strengths: Insightful, efficient, and great at giving advice (when asked).

- Communication Tip: Wait for an invitation before sharing your wisdom; otherwise, people won't hear you.

- Challenge: Feeling unseen or undervalued when people don't recognize your gifts. (They will, in time!)

5. Reflectors – The Mirrors: "I reflect the world around me and I need time to process."

- Strengths: Wise, adaptable, and deeply intuitive.

- Communication Tip: Take time before making decisions, you need space to feel what's right.

- Challenge: Avoiding environments that drain you, since you absorb energy like a sponge.

When you understand how your energy is designed to flow, you stop trying to communicate like everyone else and start expressing yourself in a way that feels natural, powerful, and true. You stop shouting to be heard and start speaking in alignment with who you really are. That's when your voice resonates. That's when people listen.

Human Design isn't about putting you in a box, it's about unlocking the box you've been stuck in. As you discover your energetic communication blueprint, give yourself permission to stop forcing and start flowing. Your voice, when expressed with energetic integrity, is your greatest tool for truth, connection, and impact. And it starts with owning *who you are.*

So take what you've learned here and begin experimenting with it. Start paying attention to how your energy shifts when you stop forcing communication and begin aligning with your natural rhythm. Notice what changes when you speak from a place of clarity rather than pressure. You may find that conversations feel easier, more authentic, and more impactful because they're finally coming from the real you.

You don't have to "perform" to be powerful, and you certainly don't need to sound like anyone else to be heard. The more you understand how your energy is designed to communicate, the more you can trust your own voice—your unique, energetic blueprint. When you stop trying to mold yourself to fit someone else's idea of expression, your truth flows naturally.

This is where your grace lives. This is where your divine expression lives. And this is where your voice becomes not just heard but deeply felt.

If you haven't gotten your Grace in Action Workbook, now is a great time to pause and get it so you can go deeper on what you've just learned and put the concepts... into action!

Go to gracesoulutions.com/workbook. You're welcome to also grab a journal you have and write your responses to the prompts that follow.

Grace Notes

Mini-Journal Prompts:

1. What Human Design type are you, and how does it resonate with the way you naturally express yourself?

2. Where in your life have you been trying to communicate like someone else and how has that felt?

3. What would it look like to speak in a way that feels aligned, honest, and natural to you?

Soul Notes

Your Human Design type reveals how your energy is meant to move through the world—and how your voice naturally wants to be heard.

Reflect on your type:

1. How does this insight help you embrace the way you communicate best?
2. Where have you been resisting or overriding your natural communication style?
3. What would it feel like to stop performing and start expressing from your energetic truth?

Let this awareness be a permission slip—not a label. The goal isn't to fit into a box, but to free your voice.

You don't have to have all the answers right now. This is about noticing the patterns, honoring your rhythm, and beginning to trust the wisdom of your energy.

Chapter 4

Own Your Emotions, Own Your Worth

Unlock the Emotional Intelligence, Confidence, and Communication Power Within You

Your emotions influence everything from how you show up in conversation to how you see yourself and claim your space in the world. Every word you speak, and even the ones you hold back, are shaped by the energy of what's going on inside you. You may not always realize it, but emotional energy speaks louder than anything else. Ever walked into a room and sensed tension before a word was said? That's emotional energy at work.

If you want to express yourself with clarity, confidence, and connection, you need more than just well-formed sentences. You need emotional presence. You have the opportunity to know what's going on inside you and how to manage that energy in real time. Otherwise, your emotions will lead the conversation, and not always in the direction you want.

That's why presence is the foundation. Emotional energy communication starts long before you speak. It begins with your energy. Your energy influences your emotional state, and together, they shape how your message is received. If you're distracted, overwhelmed, or shut down, people will sense that before you ever say a word. But when you're grounded, emotionally aware, and aligned with your energy, your communication carries clarity, presence, and impact.

I experienced this first hand at my high school graduation, a moment that should have felt triumphant. Instead, it was filled with confusion, disappointment, and a deep sense of rejection. That experience shaped how I viewed myself for years. I questioned my value. I shrank in conversations. I felt invisible. But eventually, I realized I had a choice. I could let that story keep me silent or rewrite it and reclaim my voice. I chose the latter, and it changed everything.

While emotional energy communication is what others feel from you before you speak, emotional communication is how you give voice to those feelings through your words, tone, and body language.

Emotional communication is not just about talking through feelings. It's about understanding what you're feeling, being present with it, and allowing your expression to come from truth, not reaction. When you align your emotional energy with your intention, you communicate in a way that others not only hear but feel.

Mindfulness and grounding are powerful tools to help you regulate your emotional energy. Breathing deeply, checking in with yourself, cutting out distractions, spending time in nature, or repeating grace-based affirmations can help you reconnect with your center. When you're grounded, your energy stabilizes, and your communication becomes more intentional.

Let's not forget that your emotional communication begins with more than words. Your body speaks too. Your posture, facial expressions, and gestures either support your message or silently sabotage it. Crossed arms may read as feeling guarded. A soft, steady gaze can convey openness. When your body language and what you have to say are in sync, people trust what you're saying. When they aren't, something feels off.

Your tone of voice matters as well. Think of tone as the emotional filter through which your words are heard. You can say "I'm fine" in a way that communicates anything but! The same goes for how fast you talk, how often you pause, and how present you are. Speaking too quickly may signal anxiety. Speaking too slowly can suggest hesitation. But when you add intentional pauses, you give your words room to land and your listener room to connect.

These tools are part of your emotional intelligence. In Chapter 1, we touched on EQ, and now we're expanding it. Emotional intelligence includes self-awareness, self-regulation, social awareness, and relationship management. These skills help you stay emotionally grounded even in difficult conversations.

Let me share a moment that taught me about emotional alchemy. Vulnerability and humor can shift energy in an instant. While working in Scotland as a speech-language pathologist, students started calling me "Toilet Lady" because my last name, Liu, sounds like "loo," which is British slang for toilet. I could have been offended. But instead, I laughed and owned it. Choosing playfulness over pain in that moment turned a potential wound into a connection. That experience later inspired my *Liu (Loo) Loo Life's Wisdom In Every Flush* card deck, a lighthearted tool born from an awkward moment!

That's what emotional confidence is about. It's not perfection. It's presence. It's being real. It's choosing to show up with your whole self, even when it's uncomfortable. Vulnerability is not weakness. It's courage in motion. And when you allow yourself to be seen, others feel safe to do the same.

Here are some rock-solid techniques to help you manage emotions in real-time so you stay in control, no matter what life throws your way.

1. Mindfulness Meditation: Become the Calm in the Chaos

Meditation isn't just for yogis, it's for anyone who wants to stop overreacting to every little thing. When you practice mindfulness, you train yourself to observe emotions without getting caught up in them.

Try This:
Take five minutes a day to sit quietly, breathe deeply, and just notice your thoughts. No judgment, no fixing. Just observe.

2. Breathing Exercises: Because Oxygen is Your Best Friend

Your breath is one of the fastest, most powerful tools you have to regulate your emotions. Deep breathing sends a signal to your nervous system that you're safe, helping calm the chaos within and shift you out of survival mode.

Try This:
Inhale slowly and deeply from your diaphragm for a count of four.
Hold your breath for four counts.
Then exhale gently and slowly for a count of six.
Repeat this cycle until you feel your emotions begin to settle.

Your breath is always available to support you. Take your time. If you go too fast, you may start to hyperventilate, which defeats the purpose.

3. Cognitive Reframing: Flip the Script

Your thoughts shape your emotional reality. If you constantly tell yourself, I'm not good enough or They're judging me, you'll start to believe it and feel it. But when you shift the narrative, you shift your experience.

Try This:
When a negative thought pops up, reframe it with truth and self-compassion.
Instead of, '*I'm terrible at this,*' try, '*I'm still learning, and every step counts.*'
Instead of, '*They probably think I'm awkward,*' say, '*I'm showing up as myself, and that's enough.*'

Your brain believes what you tell it. Choose words that empower you.

4. Move Your Body: Shake Off the Stress

Emotions are energy in motion. When you're feeling overwhelmed, stuck, or scattered, movement can help you reset. Physical activity helps release tension, boosts your mood, and clears mental fog.

Try This: Take a short walk, stretch, flow through some gentle yoga, or dance it out like nobody's watching. Moving your body reconnects you to your power and yes, blasting your favorite hype song is highly encouraged!

Emotional presence doesn't mean you're always calm or always in control. It means being able to recognize what's stirring beneath the surface and having the tools to bring yourself back to center when emotions run high. Often, this begins with understanding what triggers you emotionally. Those sensitive spots shaped by past experiences or long-held beliefs can hijack your energy without warning. Maybe it's a tone of voice, a particular phrase, or the way someone questions your ideas. Suddenly, you're not just reacting to the moment, you're reacting to everything that moment brings up.

When you start noticing these emotional patterns, you take the first step toward shifting them. Triggers lose their power when they are met with awareness. Instead of spiraling, you can pause, ground, and choose how you want to respond. That's resilience. And it's something you build over time. Practices like mindfulness meditation, breathing exercises, and even physical movement help shift your emotional state and reset your nervous system.

Confidence doesn't come from pretending to have it all together. It comes from knowing how to support yourself emotionally and showing up with intention. Your emotional energy sets the tone. When you manage it with care, you communicate with clarity and grace.

And that is power.

If you haven't gotten your Grace in Action Workbook, now is a great time to pause and get it so you can go deeper on what you've just learned and put the concepts... into action!

Go to gracesoulutions.com/workbook. You're welcome to also grab a journal you have and write your responses to the prompts that follow.

Grace Notes

Mini-Journal Prompts:

1. Where in your life does your emotional energy feel most aligned? Where does it feel most reactive?

2. How do your tone, body language, and pacing impact your message?

3. What tools help you return to emotional presence when you feel thrown off?

Soul Notes:

When was the last time your body said something your mouth didn't?

What would it look like to bring your voice, your truth, and your body into full alignment—without apology?

Confidence doesn't come from pretending to have it all together.

Chapter 5

Speak with Worth: Confidence, Vulnerability, and the Power of Self-Compassion

Speak Up, Worthy One. Confidence Begins Within.

You can't speak with true confidence if you don't believe in your worth. You can have the best words, the strongest points, and still feel like an imposter if you're carrying the weight of self-doubt. And here's the truth: many of us are.

We've been conditioned to believe worthiness is something we have to earn, prove, or wait for someone else to grant us. That's a lie. You were born worthy. The moment you believe that, everything begins to shift. You stop apologizing for your presence. You stop second-guessing your ideas. You stop shrinking.

Self-doubt is sneaky. It shows up in silence, in rambling, in hesitation. It convinces you to play small, to justify your ideas, or to let others take the spotlight. Awareness is the first step to shifting that.

51

The antidote to self-doubt isn't perfection. It's self-compassion. You can't hate yourself into confidence. But you can choose to speak to yourself like someone who matters. And when your inner dialogue changes, your outer expression follows.

Here are tools that help you cultivate that confidence:

Affirmations anchor you. Choose one and speak it aloud daily. "My voice matters." "I take up space with grace." "I am enough exactly as I am." Let those words replace the inner critic. Say them like you mean it, and feel their power as they leave your lips.

Energy clearing helps you release stuck emotional residue. Try breathwork, tapping, or even shaking out your hands after a difficult conversation.

Visualization prepares your brain and body for success. Picture yourself walking into a room, grounded, open, and confident. Let your imagination create the version of you who already owns their voice and then embody her.

Gratitude shifts your focus. In place of noticing what's missing, honor what's already strong. Each day, reflect on a moment where you showed up with courage or clarity, even in small ways.

Vulnerability is your strength. Let's rewrite that narrative. When you speak honestly, when you show up as you are, people connect with you not because you're perfect, but because you're real. Vulnerability builds trust, deepens relationships, and helps you own your impact without apology.

When you embrace your vulnerability, you open the door to transforming self-doubt into confidence. Self-doubt is that quiet, nagging voice that questions your worth, your readiness, your right to take up space. It slips in when you least expect it, convincing you to hold back, delay, or stay silent. Recognizing it isn't enough. You have to rewire it.

One of the most powerful ways to build confidence is to get honest about what triggers your self-doubt. What kinds of situations make you shrink? What words or looks make you question yourself? When do you feel your voice getting shaky or your energy withdrawing?

When you name those moments, you strip them of their power. Self-awareness is your first line of defense, and with it, you're able to disrupt the patterns and rebuild your communication from a place of truth. Confidence doesn't mean never feeling doubt again. It means moving forward anyway, grounded in the belief that you are worthy, that you belong, that your voice matters.

And yes, there will be hard conversations. You will face discomfort, especially with people you love. The way you navigate those moments defines the strength of your communication. I know this deeply. My husband and I had to have a raw conversation about divorce. We chose emotional presence rather than defensiveness. We listened. We validated. We stayed with the discomfort instead of running from it. And that conversation strengthened our relationship in ways we never expected.

When you lead with EQ and worthiness, even the hardest moments become opportunities for connection, clarity, and healing.

If you haven't gotten your Grace in Action Workbook, now is a great time to pause and get it so you can go deeper on what you've just learned and put the concepts... into action!

Go to gracesoulutions.com/workbook. You're welcome to also grab a journal you have and write your responses to the prompts that follow.

Grace Notes

Mini-Journal Prompts:

1. What triggers your self-doubt, and how does it affect your voice?

2. How can you show yourself more compassion in moments of vulnerability?

3. What truth are you ready to speak, even if your voice shakes?

Soul Notes:

When was the last time you silenced yourself out of fear or unworthiness?

What would it look like to revisit that moment now with self-compassion, courage, and grace?

Give yourself grace: speak
kindly to yourself, offer
compliments instead of criticism,
allow mistakes without
judgment, celebrate small wins,
and remember daily—you
matter.

Chapter 6

Own Your Awareness,
Own Your Voice

You have a voice. Now it's time to own it.

If you've ever felt like your words got stuck in your throat, like you were holding back what you really wanted to say, then this chapter is for you.

Aligning with your voice isn't just about speaking up. It's about speaking with confidence, clarity, and truth. It's about ditching the self-doubt, breaking free from old patterns, and finally communicating like the powerhouse you were born to be.

Awareness is where it all begins, it's your first step to speaking with confidence. If you don't fully know yourself, how can you expect to express yourself with confidence? When you become truly aware of who you are, your values, your truth, then your voice, your communication transforms. You will stop tiptoeing around conversations, second-guessing your words, or over-explaining just to be understood. Instead, you speak with intention and impact.

Most of us were conditioned from a young age to communicate in a certain way and with mixed messages. We were told to not interrupt, to not be loud, to say thank you and sorry. We're told that keeping quiet keeps the peace. As women, we're taught from a very early age that it's better to shrink yourself down, to become virtually invisible, and fit into other people's expectations of us.

You aren't, and I'm not, really no one is going to be palatable to everyone. That would be impossible. The truth is that your real voice has never gone anywhere. It's waiting for you to hit the Unmute button.

Aligning with your voice will have many benefits and a positive impact on all areas of your life. You will discover:

1. Perfection is the Enemy of Confidence

If you've been holding back because you're afraid of saying the "wrong" thing, here's your wake-up call: perfection simply doesn't exist. Trying to craft the perfect sentence? Exhausting. Overthinking every word before you speak? Draining. Editing yourself to fit what others want to hear? Absolutely soul-sucking. What's far more powerful than being perfect is being real. The next time you catch yourself hesitating, ask: '*Am I trying to be perfect, or am I trying to be honest? Would I rather be polished or powerful?*' Authenticity always leaves a deeper impact than perfection. Always.

2. You Are Meant to Evolve (So Stop Trying to "Lock In" One Version of Yourself)

Here's something people don't talk about enough: you are allowed to grow. What you believed five years ago may not align with what you believe now, and that's a good thing. Your voice, your confidence, and the way you express yourself are all meant to evolve. So if you've ever said, "That's just not me," or "I've never been someone who speaks up," it's time to let that story go. You are not required to stay stuck in an outdated version of yourself. Growth is the goal. Change is freedom. If you're evolving, you're doing it right.

3. Your Values Are Your North Star

If you want to communicate with ease and confidence, you need to know what you stand for. When your words align with your core values, clarity comes naturally. Ask yourself: '*What do I believe in? What are my non-negotiables?*' Are you adjusting your message to make others comfortable, or are you speaking from your own truth? When your words match your values, the need for overthinking fades. You stop explaining yourself to people who were never meant to understand you and start speaking with conviction. And guess what? People respect that.

4. The Real Work? Speaking Your Truth Even When It's Uncomfortable

Speaking with confidence isn't always smooth or easy. Sometimes, it means saying "No", when it would be easier to say "Yes". It means disagreeing with someone you love. It means setting a boundary and actually honoring it. That's the real work. Because the alternative of constantly silencing yourself to keep the peace costs way too much. Your truth deserves to be heard, even when it shakes things up. *Especially* then.

The reality is, you're never going to be right for everyone. Not everyone is going to love what you have to say. And that's okay. You're not here to be liked by everyone. You're here to live your truth. Speak up. Own your voice. Be unapologetically YOU. Because when you do, everything changes.

Speaking up, owning your voice does not mean you're being aggressive, you're not being "too much", it means you're being assertive. Assertiveness is rooted in confidence and clarity about expressing your needs, boundaries, and beliefs with self-respect and respect for others.

Aggression, on the other hand, is about control and dominance, often at the expense of connection. The two are not the same. When you understand the difference, you can start owning your voice without apology and without fear of pushing people away. True assertiveness looks like someone who speaks clearly and confidently. They don't yell or overpower.

An assertive communicator speaks with clarity and confidence, without the need to yell, overpower, or dominate. They express their thoughts, feelings, and needs without guilt or apology, and they listen to others without losing their own voice. Assertiveness is the balance between standing your ground and respecting someone else's perspective. It means being able to say "No" without over-explaining and "Yes" without hesitation. It's not about shrinking to make others comfortable or bulldozing to be heard.

It's about standing tall in your truth and owning your voice with grace and power.

The aggressive communicator talks over people instead of listening. An aggressive communicator often uses blame-heavy language like "You always..." or "You never...," putting others on the defensive and shutting down meaningful dialogue. They tend to steamroll conversations, speaking over others rather than creating space for real discussion. Instead of listening or considering different perspectives, they operate from the belief that they're always right and dismissing or devaluing opposing views. Imagine someone snapping, "You never listen to me or you're always too busy," without giving the other person a chance to respond. That's aggression in action. It doesn't foster connection. It breeds resentment. Aggression burns bridges. Assertiveness, on the other hand, builds them.

I once had a co-worker who would take over every conversation. They'd steamroll over me, speaking non-stop without leaving any room for questions, discussion, or alternate opinions. It wasn't just frustrating; it was exhausting. Over time, I found myself dreading meetings and second-guessing my input, even when I knew I had something valuable to contribute. It left me feeling tired, worn out, and worthless, like my voice didn't matter. That's what aggressive communication does. It doesn't just dominate a space, it drains the people in it. And here's the thing: it didn't make them more respected. It made them avoided. True influence doesn't come from control. It comes from presence, respect, and the kind of confidence that invites conversation rather than shuts it down.

If you've been conditioned to be nice, to not rock the boat, or just go with the flow, standing firm in your voice might feel uncomfortable at first.

Here's how to step into your power without losing your grace. Being assertive isn't a personality trait. It's a skill, and like any skill, it can be developed with intention and repetition. Here's how to build it into your everyday life:

1. Use "I" Statements Instead of Blame Statements

Assertiveness is about expressing your feelings without attacking someone else. When you lead with "you always" or "you never," it puts the other person on the defensive and often shuts down the conversation. "I" statements, on the other hand, invite connection and clarity.

Try This:

Instead of saying, "You never listen to me!" say, "I feel unheard when I'm interrupted."

It keeps the focus on how you feel and creates space for resolution, not resistance.

2. Stand Tall, Speak Steady

Your presence speaks before your words ever do. Your posture, tone, and energy tell the story of how confident (or uncertain) you feel. Grounding yourself physically can instantly elevate how people receive your message.

Try This:

Relax your shoulders, stand or sit tall, and avoid fidgeting. Take a breath before you speak to slow down your delivery.

When you're calm and grounded, people are more likely to listen and trust what you say. (Remember those grounding exercises? Now's the time to use them.)

3. Embrace the Power of the Pause

You don't have to fill every moment of silence with nervous chatter. A pause, when used intentionally, can become one of your most powerful communication tools.

Try This:

Pause before you respond. Let your words land. Allow silence to do some of the heavy lifting.

A well-placed pause makes you sound more intentional, gives others time to process, and shows that you're not rushing to defend yourself. Silence isn't awkward. It's powerful. Own it.

4. Role-Play with a Friend

Role-playing may feel awkward at first, but it's one of the fastest ways to build confidence in real-life situations.

Try This:
Ask a trusted friend to role-play scenarios like asking for a raise, setting a boundary with a loved one, or saying no without overexplaining.

Bonus: switch roles. Seeing both sides builds empathy and deepens your communication confidence.

5. Practice Assertiveness in Everyday Moments

You don't need a major confrontation to practice assertiveness. Start with the small, everyday moments that usually go unnoticed.

Try This:
Order your food confidently (ditch the "Umm, I guess..."). Speak first in a group even if your voice shakes, and ask for what you want without apologizing.

These micro-moments add up and gradually rewire how you show up.

6. Self-Advocacy in Professional Settings

Speaking up in a professional environment can feel intimidating, but it's a key area where assertiveness can help you stand out in the best way.

Try This:
Prepare your key points before meetings. If you're interrupted, say, "I'd like to finish my thought." Replace apologetic language like "Sorry, but..." with "I believe this is the best approach because..."

Small tweaks, big power shifts.

7. Ask for Feedback

Sometimes the best way to grow is to ask a mentor. Feedback gives you insight into how others perceive your communication and how you can refine it.

Try This:
Ask a mentor, friend, or colleague: "Do I come across as confident, or do I soften my words too much?" Their observations might reveal blind spots or strengths you hadn't even noticed.

Wendie's story is a masterclass in what happens when you're out of alignment with your voice, and how avoiding confrontation can create unnecessary stress.

Wendie is a good friend and former colleague. At the time of this incident, we were no longer working together, but she shared the experience with me afterward. A colleague nicknamed her "Two-Space Wendie," teasing her for leaving two spaces after a period in emails. What seemed like a harmless joke to others felt like a subtle dig to Wendie. Instead of addressing it directly, she held it in, stewed over it, and eventually complained to their boss, who, unfortunately, was also the colleague's friend. The stress built, not because of the comment itself, but because she didn't feel safe or empowered to speak up.

And what did that accomplish? More tension. More awkwardness. More stress.

Wendie's response wasn't direct. It was passive-aggressive. She began ignoring her colleague when he tried to make small talk and shut down instead of opening a conversation. The work environment grew cold and tense, not because of the job itself, but because of the unspoken friction between them. Eventually, she quit. It wasn't because of the workload, but because of the emotional toll of unresolved tension. Sound familiar?

Many people fear confrontation so much they'd rather bottle things up, vent to everyone but the person involved, or quietly withdraw and hope the issue disappears. Spoiler alert: it never does. Avoidance doesn't create peace; it creates pressure.

Wendie wasn't wrong for feeling annoyed or wanting to be respected. But she gave away her power by not addressing the issue directly. Instead of saying, "Hey, I know you think it's funny, but the nickname bothers me. Can we drop it?" she let the frustration build until walking away felt easier than speaking up. She knew assertiveness was a challenge. She could advocate fiercely for others but froze when it came to herself. This was something rooted in how she was raised to fear confrontation.

Wendie was aware of her struggle, but she wasn't ready to change it, and that was her choice. Awareness doesn't always require immediate action; it means recognizing what's happening and taking responsibility for how you respond. I could have encouraged her to confront her colleague, but it wasn't my choice to make. She saw her options clearly and chose what felt right in that moment.

That's the key. Awareness gives you the power to choose. Some people will step up and speak their truth. Others, like Wendie, might choose to walk away. Neither path is right or wrong, as long as it comes from awareness, not fear. Because the real problem is not choosing at all.

Effective communication isn't just about choosing the right words, it's about owning your message, building connection, and honoring mutual respect. First, let's talk about clarity. If you've ever rambled through a conversation and walked away thinking, '*What was I even trying to say?*' you're not alone. That's what happens when you speak without first getting clear. Before opening your mouth, pause and ask yourself: '*What's my core message? What outcome do I want from this conversation? Am I speaking from confidence or fear?*'

When you're grounded in your truth, your words carry weight. Next comes connection because communication is a two-way street. Talking at someone is a monologue; real communication is an exchange. Listen deeply, acknowledge emotions, and ask better questions. Want to be heard? Make others feel heard first.

And finally, respect. Assertive communication is not about steamrolling others. You can be clear and direct without being harsh. Speak your truth with intention, not volume, and you'll lead conversations with both power and grace.

Even the best communicators can fall into the trap of assuming instead of asking, and that's where so much unnecessary stress begins. You assume someone is upset because their reply was short. You assume your idea was rejected because there was no immediate feedback. You assume others should just know what you need without telling them. And then? You spiral. You overthink. You let doubt creep in. We've all done it. But assumptions create confusion; asking creates clarity.

So let's stop playing mind reader. If something feels off, ask. If you're unsure, ask. If you need more information, ask. Because asking doesn't make you needy or weak. It makes you empowered.

And if you've ever felt like you weren't worthy of asking for clarity, I get it. I used to live there too. I didn't realize it at the time, but deep down I believed I wasn't worthy of peace of mind, that I didn't deserve answers. If you'd asked me back then, I wouldn't have admitted it. But the truth is, your voice matters. Your peace matters. You are worthy of clarity. That's what The *Pearl of Grace* is all about: using your voice, asking the questions, and choosing truth over assumption, because nothing less than that will do.

There are techniques that you can practice and put into place to ensure your communication is powerful, not aggressive. Together with your newfound clarity and assertiveness, this will be a game changer for you.

When you practice active listening, you give people your full attention. Nod, paraphrase their words, and ask clarifying questions. Ask open-ended questions instead of questions that can be answered with a simple "Yes" or "No". Encourage deeper conversation with prompts like, "What sparked that feeling for you?" or "How do you see this situation evolving?"

Validate feelings. Acknowledge emotions, your own or others'. Promote understanding and connection through phrases like, "I can see that this is important to you," to foster stronger ties.

Emotional awareness plays an important part in communication. This is how it shows up in your voice. Being aware helps you strengthen how you speak and how you respond.

Your emotions influence how you communicate. When you don't understand your emotions, you might get defensive instead of discussing, over-explain instead of standing firm, or shut down instead of expressing your needs.

Before speaking, ask yourself: What emotions am I bringing into this conversation? Am I reacting out of habit, or responding with intention? Is this about the present moment, or is an old wound being triggered?

Awareness is power. When you understand your emotions, you control your communication, not the other way around.

Notice your triggers. What always sets you off? A dismissive tone? Feeling unheard? Being criticized? These reactions are rooted in past experiences. When you identify your triggers, you can break the pattern instead of repeating it.

Trace your emotional reactions to their source. If talking about your successes makes you uncomfortable, ask yourself: Was I raised to believe that celebrating myself was bragging? Was I taught that my needs weren't as important as others'? Have I been silencing myself to keep the peace?

You weren't born doubting your voice. Somewhere along the way, you were taught to.

Now it's time to unlearn.

Awareness gives you the power to choose differently. Some scripts we carry weren't even ours to begin with. They were inherited, passed down, or absorbed from someone else's pain.

Reflect after every major conversation. Instead of replaying, "What I should have said," use the moment to grow. Ask yourself: "What did I express well? Where did I hold back? What can I do differently next time?" Awareness is the key to growth.

You can learn from people who communicate with confidence. Want to be a better communicator? Study people who do it well. Watch how they handle tough conversations. Notice how they stay calm under pressure. Learn how they set boundaries with ease. Surround yourself with people who communicate with grace and power, and you'll start embodying it too.

Speaking with confidence, as you've learned already, comes from mastering awareness. Awareness is more than just knowing yourself. It's about having the courage to own who you are, flaws, strengths, quirks, and all, and then communicating that self boldly and unapologetically. It's about recognizing patterns, rewriting limiting narratives, and standing firm in your truth without needing outside validation.

Know yourself. Get clear on your values, your energetic communication blueprint and communication style. Practice mindful listening. Communication is just as much about listening and hearing as it is about speaking. Embrace vulnerability. Expressing yourself honestly is courageous. I speak about communication styles later in the book.

Seek opportunities to grow. Read books, take courses, and surround yourself with people who inspire you. Set small communication goals. Whether it's speaking up in meetings, setting boundaries, or using fewer filler words, work on one thing at a time. Celebrate progress, not perfection. Your growth is a journey.

Every time you speak up instead of staying silent, set a boundary with confidence, or express yourself without over-explaining, you are stepping into your power. It's not about being perfect. It's about being real. Honor your voice. Communicate your truth.

And never dim yourself to make others comfortable.

Because your voice is worthy. Your truth is valuable. And the world needs to hear it.

Your emotional history plays a huge role in how you express yourself. Whether you were taught to be seen and not heard, or raised in an environment where speaking your mind was encouraged, those early experiences shaped how you communicate today.

But you're not stuck there! By understanding your emotional landscape, you can begin to rewrite the stories that no longer serve you and step fully into your voice. Think about a time when you felt truly aligned with your voice. What was happening? Who were you with? What allowed you to express yourself freely? Are there certain situations where you shut down? Or times when you over-explain?

Awareness of these patterns helps you take back control of your communication.

Sometimes, past experiences create emotional blocks that keep us silent. Awareness is the first step in releasing them. Whether it's journaling, therapy, meditation, EFT tapping, or Quantum Level Reprogramming, healing begins when you become conscious of what's holding you back. That's how your true voice starts to emerge.

Being aware doesn't mean you have to communicate the same way in every setting. It means knowing how to adapt while staying rooted in your truth. You don't talk to your boss the same way you talk to your best friend, and that isn't inauthentic—it is intentional and emotionally intelligent. The key is to be flexible without losing yourself.

You can be both professional and authentic. With awareness, you learn how to express your thoughts clearly and respectfully while being mindful of workplace dynamics. Sharing a little about yourself doesn't make you unprofessional. It makes you relatable. The best communicators know how to weave in personal truth to build trust. That doesn't mean oversharing. Awareness helps you know what to share, when, and with whom.

Real relationships thrive on honesty and vulnerability, but only when rooted in self-awareness. If you want deep, meaningful connections, you must be willing to be seen. Instead of avoiding difficult conversations, lean in with grace and discernment. A simple, "I'd love to have this conversation, but let's save it for a better time," can honor your boundaries and your truth. When you speak from a grounded place, you give others permission to do the same.

That is how trust is built. That is how relationships grow.

Every time you speak up instead of staying silent, express yourself without over-explaining, and communicate with clarity, you reinforce your worthiness. You show up more fully and prove to yourself that your voice matters.

Because it darn well does.

You are worthy of being heard. You are worthy of taking up space. And the more aware you become of who you are and how you communicate, the more confident and grounded your voice becomes.

Authentic communication is not about being perfect. It is about being real. And real begins with awareness. That is where the magic starts.

If you haven't gotten your Grace in Action Workbook, now is a great time to pause and get it so you can go deeper on what you've just learned and put the concepts... into action!

Go to gracesoulutions.com/workbook. You're welcome to also grab a journal you have and write your responses to the prompts that follow.

Grace Notes

Mini-Journal Prompts:

1. Describe a moment where you spoke your truth with confidence. What made it possible and how did it feel?

2. Identify a situation or relationship where your voice shrinks. What story are you telling yourself in that space?

3. Not someday—today. What's one small action you can take to speak up with more presence and power?

Soul Notes:

Write your own personal Mission Statement. Include:

1. Who are you?
2. What do you stand for?
3. What kind of communicator do you want to be?

Having a mission statement helps guide your interactions and keeps you grounded in your truth.

When you become truly aware
of who you are, your values,
your truth, your voice, your
communication transforms.

Chapter 7

Own Your Resilience, Own Your Confidence

Rooted in Resilience, Radiating Confidence

Resilience is our ability to recover, reset, and keep moving forward. It's the capacity we have to withstand or bounce back quickly from difficulties. Life isn't a straight, smooth road. It's winding, unpredictable, and filled with detours, potholes, and obstacles.

As you've read so far, many of our obstacles aren't external. We create them through our own lack of confidence, our negative inner voice, and emotional dysregulation. The good news? You've also learned you can recover, reset, and keep moving forward.

What does resilience have to do with confidence? Plenty. Why does it matter in my communication? Again, plenty. Resilience and confidence are a package deal. When you build resilience, confidence follows. When you radiate confidence, you inspire trust, respect, and stronger connections. Together, these two qualities shape your ability to communicate effectively, bounce back from challenges, and own your voice.

That's why resilience and confidence aren't just related, they're interdependent. One feeds the other, and together they give your voice its strength.

Resilience often begins when you face the hard stuff head-on. For me, that moment came in college, when I had to admit to myself and others that my chosen path wasn't the right one.

I was studying pharmacy because I thought I was supposed to. My grandfather was a pharmacist, and I wanted to follow in his footsteps, or at least I thought I did. It was a stable career. It made sense. My dad was proud I was continuing the family legacy. It ticked all the right boxes.

But then I hit a massive roadblock: physics. No matter how hard I tried, I just couldn't get it. I felt like I was drowning, grasping for understanding, and sinking deeper each time I reached for a lifeline.

Then came the meeting with my academic advisor that sealed my fate: I wasn't going to make it through pharmacy school. But the hardest conversation? Telling my parents. My dad was crushed. His disappointment wasn't subtle. He stopped talking to me for three months. And let me tell you, silence is its own language, and a painful one.

Silence didn't bring peace. It brought disconnection—from others and from myself.

Silence is not the enemy, but it's not always your ally either.

Silence can be sacred. It can hold space for emotion, presence, reflection. It can let your energy speak louder than words. In a heated moment, intentional silence can be a power move, an anchor that grounds the room.

But silence can also be avoidance. A way to withdraw, disappear, or shut down. Sometimes it's mistaken for grace when it's actually fear or discomfort.

When silence feels awkward, don't rush to fill it. Lean in. Ask yourself: Is something unsaid lingering in the space? If so, that's an invitation for repair or clarification.

As you grow more aware of your voice, become more aware of your silences too. Are they chosen with power, or defaulted out of fear? But in that silence, I found clarity. I refused to let this one failure define me. I had a choice: wallow in disappointment or get creative with my future. So, what did I do?

I grabbed a dartboard. Yes, an actual dartboard. I wrote down a bunch of potential majors, pinned them around the board, and let three darts decide my fate.

The results? Marine Biology. Psychology. Speech-Language Pathology.

With those three options, I did my research, followed my interests, and trusted my gut. Speech-language pathology won out. I didn't fully realize it was the right choice until my grandfather had a stroke. Watching him work with a speech therapist and witnessing firsthand how communication could be rebuilt sealed my decision. It was my calling all along. I just needed a creative way to find it.

Eventually, my dad came around. He became one of my biggest supporters. This journey taught me a powerful truth: resilience isn't about *never* falling. It's about how you rise after you do.

A weak resilience muscle shows up in your communication when you're misunderstood, or you feel misunderstood. Some days, our words flow like poetry, and other days, we're a clunky mess of over-explaining, awkward pauses, and misinterpretations. In some cases, we hold on to what we want to say for fear of what others will think. We bottle it up, beat ourselves up over it because we don't want to mess up. We don't bounce back, we don't recover. Instead of having CONFIDENCE in ourselves and our communication, we shut down.

Spoiler alert: Beating yourself up over it doesn't make you a better communicator. It just keeps you stuck in self-doubt.

Resilience isn't perfection. Perfection, as we know, doesn't exist. Being resilient means you're flexible, adaptable, and steady through setbacks. It's a muscle. The more you use it, the stronger it becomes.

Every strong communicator has stumbled over their words, felt misunderstood, or regretted something they said. The difference between them and those who stay silent or shrink?

Resilience.

Resilience helps you recover from slip-ups without spiraling. It helps you handle criticism without letting it shake you. It helps you stay grounded when conversations get messy. It turns communication breakdowns into growth moments. And it's not something you're born with. It's something you build.

So how do you build it? Through experience. Through practice. Through those awkward, uncomfortable, even cringe-worthy moments where you keep showing up and keep trying.

Before you can navigate communication detours with confidence, you need to understand what knocks you off course. What triggers you? What makes you shut down or get defensive? What causes you to over-explain, avoid, or overcompensate?

These aren't flaws. They're insights. Self-awareness isn't about judgment. It's about clarity. It's how you pause and choose a better response instead of reacting on autopilot.

Think of it like this: You can't fix a leaky faucet if you don't know where the drip is coming from. The same goes for communication patterns. When you notice where you're leaking confidence, you begin to repair it.

Start by paying close attention to your reactions during conversations. Were you rattled, silenced, or caught off guard?

Reflect on the trigger. Was it the person, the topic, or something unresolved within you? Was your nervous system dysregulated, or were you just not fully present?

Another powerful strategy? Ask for feedback. It can make you feel vulnerable, but a trusted friend, mentor, or coach can help you see what you can't. Choose someone who's honest but kind, someone who wants to see you grow.

As your awareness deepens, notice your patterns. Do you hesitate to speak in groups? Do you over-explain to authority figures or people you want to impress? These habits are often rooted in self-protection. Once you recognize them, you can shift them gently and intentionally.

Also, reflect on where your confidence thrives. Where do you speak with ease? Where does doubt creep in? Knowing your comfort zones matters.

The goal isn't to avoid discomfort. It's to stretch, not abandon, your comfort zone. Ground yourself in new spaces and you'll expand your capacity to communicate with confidence.

And here's something we don't talk about enough. Emotional regulation. Resilience isn't just about recovering after a tough conversation. It's about staying present during one. Confidence doesn't just come from hindsight. It grows when you learn how to stay emotionally centered while you are still in the moment.

Have you ever walked away from a conversation and thought, I could have said...? That's often a sign your nervous system wasn't regulated enough for your voice to come through.

Emotional regulation means pausing, breathing, and responding—instead of reacting. It doesn't mean ignoring your feelings. It means guiding them.

How do you actually stay grounded when emotions run high? Here are five go-to techniques to help you regulate in real time—no perfection required. Just presence.

The Power of the Pause: Before you blurt out words in a knee-jerk reaction, take a beat. Count to three. A pause buys you time to process your emotions, collect your thoughts, and respond with clarity instead of defensiveness.

Deep Breathing to Reset: When your emotions settle, your words carry more power. Try this: Inhale for four counts, hold for four, exhale for four, hold for four. This calms your nervous system so your brain doesn't go into fight-or-flight mode.

Physical Grounding: When tension rises, bring yourself back to the present moment. Feel your feet planted firmly on the floor. Grip something solid, a pen, the chair you're sitting on, or your own hand. This simple act keeps you from spiraling into overthinking.

Emotional Checkpoints: During a conversation, do a self-check. Without removing yourself, notice how you are speaking. Is it with confidence or are you reacting out of fear? If it's fear, take a breath and reset. You're in control of how your message is delivered.

Tabling the Topic When Necessary: Not every conversation needs an immediate resolution. If a discussion is getting heated, it's okay to take a step back. Try saying, "I want to give this the attention it deserves. Can we continue this when we've both had time to reflect?" This prevents impulsive reactions and allows space for more thoughtful communication.

Building resilience isn't about getting it right every time; it's about returning to your power when things go sideways. It means giving yourself permission to be human. Sometimes you will stumble. Sometimes you will say the wrong thing or fumble through an interaction. That is part of the process.

It's about trusting that even when your voice shakes, you still have something worth saying. And when you approach conversations with resilience and confidence, you stop living in fear of missteps and start showing up with presence, clarity, and strength.

And remember, how you talk to yourself matters—it's the power of self-compassion. It means being your own best friend. That voice in your head can either fuel your confidence or erode it. Make it your ally, not your enemy. If a friend told you they messed up a conversation, would you scold them? Or would you remind them of their effort, their courage, and their heart? Offer yourself that same grace.

Instead of saying, "I sounded so awkward," try saying, "I showed up and spoke my truth. Next time, I will refine it." Instead of thinking, They probably thought I was a mess, reframe it to, I did my best, and that is enough. Self-kindness does not make you "soft". It makes you stronger.

Every time you choose to respond to yourself with care instead of criticism, you reinforce your awareness and resilience. You affirm that mistakes are part of the process of mastery. Confidence is not about avoiding failure. It is about knowing you can bounce back again and again.

Confidence isn't loud, and resilience isn't rigid. They're both rooted in your willingness to keep showing up, to learn forward, and to trust yourself a little more each time. You don't need to be perfect. You just need to be present, be curious, and keep going.

You're more resilient than you know.

And with every conversation, you're becoming more confident, more grounded, and more you.

If you haven't gotten your Grace in Action Workbook, now is a great time to pause and get it so you can go deeper on what you've just learned and put the concepts... into action!

Go to gracesoulutions.com/workbook. You're welcome to also grab a journal you have and write your responses to the prompts that follow.

Grace Notes

Mini-Journal Prompts:

1. Think of a time you bounced back from a setback, especially in communication. What did you learn about your strength?

2. Where do you feel least confident when speaking up? Explore the patterns or fears that come up in those moments. What shift would help you feel more grounded?

3. What does confidence feel like in your body and energy? Describe how you show up when you feel resilient, grounded, and fully yourself. How can you access that version of you more often?

Soul Notes:

How can you support yourself the next time a conversation doesn't go as planned? Try one of the five go-to techniques listed in this chapter.

What difference did you feel?

Resilience doesn't mean perfection—perfection doesn't exist.

Chapter 8

Resilience in Action

Speak Boldly, Even When It's Hard

Life will throw challenges your way, but resilience isn't about never falling. It's about rising again with confidence. As you've seen, awareness helps you recognize what's happening within yourself during tough moments, while assertiveness gives you the strength to express yourself clearly. Together, they lay the foundation for resilient communication. But what happens when a conversation turns awkward, emotions run high, or things don't go as planned?

That's where resilience steps in.

Resilience isn't about bouncing back. It's about staying grounded in discomfort, responding instead of reacting, and handling tough conversations with grace. Not every interaction will go smoothly, and that's okay. Resilience means knowing that one difficult moment doesn't define a relationship.

Different environments bring different communication dynamics. Professional, social, and family settings each require their own level of awareness and adaptability. You likely don't speak to your best friend the way you do to a coworker, and for good reason. Navigating conversations with confidence across different settings means strengthening your resilience muscle.

In personal relationships, whether with family, friends, or partners, the emotional stakes can feel higher. You're not just exchanging ideas—you're exchanging trust, vulnerability, and care. That's why resilient communication in personal settings requires empathy, boundaries, and emotional self-awareness.

Setting Boundaries:

Communicating what you need without guilt is a resilience superpower. Setting boundaries respectfully means being clear and firm about your needs while maintaining kindness and compassion. It's not about confrontation. It's about connection. You might say, "Thank you for understanding, but I'm not ready to talk about this right now," or "I'd like to continue this conversation when we're both calm and can listen to each other." By focusing on your feelings and using "I" statements, you take responsibility for your needs without blaming or shaming the other person.

Respectful boundaries protect your energy, foster healthier relationships, and are a quiet yet powerful act of resilience.

Handling Tough Talks with Loved Ones:

Whether it's a disagreement with a partner, a hard conversation with family, or addressing a long-standing issue, resilience helps you communicate openly without fear. Start by grounding yourself.

Breathe, center your thoughts, and remind yourself that your goal is to connect, not to confront. Use calm, clear language and "I" statements to express your feelings without blame, such as "I feel hurt when..." or "I want us to find a better way to talk about this." Listen with openness, even when it's difficult, and allow space for the other person's perspective. Resilience helps you stay present rather than purely reactive. You can face discomfort with grace and remain committed to understanding.

Navigating Emotional Triggers:
Emotional triggers can surface unexpectedly, especially in close relationships. Past wounds or unmet needs may be stirred, and resilience gives you the awareness to pause before reacting. Instead of shutting down or lashing out, try saying, "I would like a moment to process this," or "This is bringing up a lot for me and I'd like to revisit it when I'm feeling more grounded." Owning your emotions and communicating them with care creates space for healing and connection. Resilience doesn't mean never getting triggered. It means knowing how to respond with intention when you are.

Resilience in the workplace and other professional settings is just as vital. It helps you speak up, receive feedback, and navigate conflict without losing your center. While professional settings often call for more structured communication, the same emotional principles apply. Clarity, presence, and emotional regulation still matter.

Speaking Up in Meetings:
Using your voice in professional settings can feel intimidating, especially if you're more reserved, or if self-doubt sneaks in. But resilience reminds you that courage isn't about being fearless. It's about showing up anyway. Speaking up, even when your voice shakes, is a powerful act of presence. Start small: ask a question, share a quick insight, or support a colleague's idea. Each time you contribute, you reinforce your confidence and show that your perspective matters.

Growth doesn't happen in silence. It happens in action.

Handling Criticism:

Receiving criticism can sting, especially when you care deeply about your work. Resilient communication helps you separate your worth from the feedback. Ask yourself, "What part of this helps me grow?" Not all feedback is helpful, so use discernment. Take what serves you and let the rest go. Respond with calm professionalism: "Thank you for the feedback. I'll reflect on that." This approach shows emotional maturity and leaves the door open for collaboration. Criticism doesn't have to crush you. With resilience, it becomes fuel for refinement.

Navigating Workplace Conflict:

Conflict in the workplace is inevitable but it doesn't have to be destructive. Resilient communicators approach tension with a solution-oriented mindset. Instead of blaming, try: "Let's look at how we can move forward" or "Help me understand your perspective so we can find common ground." Curiosity diffuses defensiveness and invites cooperation. Resilience lets you rise above the drama, leading with emotional intelligence, clarity, and purpose.

Sometimes you'll get it wrong. There will be moments of self-doubt. Some conversations won't go as planned. None of that means you're not worthy of being heard.

What matters most is that you keep going.

Every time you pause instead of react, express yourself even when it's uncomfortable, recover from miscommunication without spiraling, and stand firm in your truth without overexplaining, you're strengthening your resilience. That's what makes you a powerful communicator.

Your voice deserves to be heard. Your experiences deserve to be honored.

And your confidence? It's already within you. You just need to tap into it.

Here's what I want you to remember: **Every conversation is an opportunity to grow.**

Every challenge makes you stronger. You are capable, powerful, and worthy of being heard.

So speak boldly. Stay rooted. And let your resilience shine.

If you haven't gotten your Grace in Action Workbook, now is a great time to pause and get it so you can go deeper on what you've just learned and put the concepts... into action!

Go to gracesoulutions.com/workbook. You're welcome to also grab a journal you have and write your responses to the prompts that follow.

Grace Notes

Mini-Journal Prompts:

1. Reflect on a recent difficult conversation you had. How did you respond? What could you do differently in future conversations to handle them with more resilience and grace?

2. Think of a time when you needed to set a boundary but felt guilty or unsure. How did you express your needs, and how did the other person respond?

3. Identify a situation where you were emotionally triggered during a conversation. How did you react, and what would you have done differently if you had paused before responding?

Soul Notes:

Take time to explore a challenging moment in both a personal and professional setting where resilience was tested. In each case, ask yourself:

1. How did I handle the situation?
2. What emotional triggers surfaced, and...
3. How did I respond?

Resilient communicators don't dwell on problems— they find solutions.

Chapter 9

Commitment to Growth: Strengthen Your Communication Superpowers

Growth Happens in the Stretch

Awareness, emotional regulation, and assertiveness are the foundations of empowered communication. Reworking these areas in your life shows a commitment to growth and to honoring your truth. But how do you take what you've learned so far and expand your communication even further?

That is what this chapter is all about: Leveling up.

No one wakes up as a flawless communicator who always knows exactly what to say, when to say it, or how to deliver it with impact. Great communicators are not born. They are built through intention, presence, and practice. Communication mastery comes from showing up, even when it feels downright messy. It comes from learning through real-life conversations and being willing to grow, fumble, reflect, and always try again.

The most magnetic communicators do not get every interaction right. They trust themselves to stay grounded and connected. Even in high-pressure moments, they hold their center, speak with clarity, and respond with calm. That kind of confidence comes from knowing they can handle whatever arises.

Communication confidence grows through experience. You learn how to navigate messy conversations by being in them! Let go of aiming for perfection and lean into practice. Each moment you stretch your voice, even with trembling words, is a step toward a powerful presence.

Growth rarely lives in your comfort zone. If you want to communicate with confidence, stretch yourself. Speak up even when your voice shakes. Initiate the complicated conversation. Set a boundary without explaining it away. Say "No" without guilt. These are not just acts of bravery. They are communication workouts that build your strength.

Discomfort is a sign that you are expanding.

Great communicators are students first. They keep learning. They observe others, read, listen, and stay curious. They surround themselves with feedback and growth. So, why not watch TED Talks? Read books that challenge your beliefs. Seek out speakers who inspire you. Better yet, get coached or mentored. Join a masterclass, like mine, where you can sharpen your skills in real time with others on the same journey.

Do you want to become a dynamic communicator? Step outside the echo chamber. Talk to people with different experiences, cultural backgrounds, and beliefs. Every new perspective stretches you. It teaches you to adapt your voice and language. The more diverse your conversations, the more flexible your communication becomes.

Who inspires you with their presence and words? Think of that friend who can navigate tough talks with ease. That speaker who moves you to tears. That leader who commands respect with calm. Watch them. Learn from their body language, tone, and energy. Pick up what resonates. You do not need to "copy" them. Simply integrate elements from their style that strengthens your own voice. Eventually, you can become the example others look to.

Strengthening your communication muscle is not just about how you speak, verbalise. It is also about how you connect. Leading with openness and authenticity invites meaningful conversations and builds trust.

Trust is built through consistency. Show up. Follow through. Let your relationships deepen through vulnerability. Share your stories, your fears, and your dreams. Check in regularly with people who matter to you. This is not about saying the *perfect* thing. It is about staying connected.

Create safe spaces where others feel encouraged to express themselves without judgment. When you listen, and truly listen, your presence becomes a gift. Active listening validates, strengthens relationships, and reinforces the truth that communication is about connection, not control.

You are still learning. You are still growing. With practice, your communication will keep getting stronger. Let your voice be guided by your values, supported by the connections you create, and refined through every conversation you choose to enter.

You are becoming a powerful communicator.

One aligned word at a time.

If you haven't gotten your Grace in Action Workbook, now is a great time to pause and get it so you can go deeper on what you've just learned and put the concepts... into action!

Go to gracesoulutions.com/workbook. You're welcome to also grab a journal you have and write your responses to the prompts that follow.

Grace Notes

Mini Journal Prompts:

1. Write down a negative thought you've had after a recent interaction. Now rewrite it with self-compassion and encouragement. How does the new version make you feel?

2. Describe a conversation or moment that didn't go the way you wanted. What can you learn from it? Take what you learned and write yourself a short forgiveness note. What would you say if this were your best friend?

3. Recall a time when you held back from speaking up. What stopped you? What would it feel like to give yourself permission to speak freely next time?

Soul Notes:

List three recent communication "wins." These can be as simple as speaking up, setting a boundary, or staying calm.

How do these moments reflect the communicator you're becoming?

Being resilient doesn't mean
getting it right every time.
It means giving yourself
permission to be human.

Chapter 10

Own Your Love,
Own Your Healing

The Power of Love in Communication

Love is the foundation of meaningful relationships and powerful communication. It's what deepens connections, fosters understanding, and builds trust. When we communicate with love, we create a safe space for openness, vulnerability, and authenticity. In this space, words are spoken not just to be heard, but to be felt and understood.

Communicating with love does not mean avoiding conflict. It doesn't mean sugarcoating the truth or tiptoeing around difficult conversations. It means choosing to approach every interaction with the intention of understanding, rather than simply reacting.

This chapter, the last part of PEARL, will show you how to use love as a tool to strengthen communication, especially when things break down. Breakdowns are going to happen. But learning how to repair with love is where the magic happens.

Love in communication isn't about romance or affection. It's about intention. It's about choosing understanding over ego, connection over winning, and growth over being right. Love builds empathy. It encourages active listening. It invites compassion over judgment. When love leads, you listen with your heart. You soften the need to be right and instead lean into grace.

You offer presence, not just words. And when you do that, conversations transform.

Love strengthens communication by building empathy. You begin to listen not just to the words, but to the emotions underneath. You pay attention to body language, tone, and silence. You look for what's not being said and meet it with care.

Love also encourages active listening. It keeps you present. No formulating your response mid-conversation. No tuning out because you think you already know. Love means you're listening to understand, not just to reply. You give someone the gift of your full presence, which says: "*I see you. You matter.*"

Love softens judgment. You don't rush to correct or criticize. You pause. You lean into grace. You remember that nobody's perfect. Not *you*. Not *them*. And in that moment, you choose connection over control. You create no-judgment zones in your relationships, spaces where people can speak their truth and know they'll be met with compassion.

Love fosters emotional safety. Ever felt like you were walking on eggshells? That's what happens when love is missing from communication. But when love leads, it says: "You're safe here. You can show up as you are. And your voice matters."

Let me tell you a story. The day I became The Devil Woman. It was during a travel assignment. I had exactly one week between jobs and a long list of things to get done. So I did what I do best. I made a detailed to-do list for my husband, Norman. Bullet points. Sub-steps. Bolded words. You name it.

Norman, on the other hand, was completely unfazed. And just when I was about to snap, he taped a picture of me to the cabinet. With Devil horns! Right next to a drawing of himself crying, with cartoonish snot dripping down his nose.

Now, I could have exploded! But instead, I laughed. Because I knew what he was doing. Norman's communication style is humor. It's his pressure valve. It's how he says, "You're coming on too strong and I'm shutting down."

Mine? I'm a nurturer. I give details, support, and structure. But that day, I crossed into smothering. His drawing was his playful, loving way of saying, "Back off a little." And because I knew his style, I didn't take it as an insult. I took it as a cue. I laughed, paused, adjusted, and we had an actual conversation.

That's the power of love in communication. It's not just about what we say. It's about how we see each other. It's knowing your partner's or friend's or colleague's style well enough to interpret the intention behind their message. Love helps you take things less personally and more compassionately.

Even a Devil horns drawing can become a tool for connection when love is leading the way.

Now let's talk about what happens when connection breaks down, because it will. Whether it's a snappy text, a misread tone, or a full-blown argument, rupture is inevitable. What matters is your ability to repair.

Repair isn't about a polished apology. It's about showing up with humility and saying, "That didn't land the way I hoped. Can we talk about it?" It's about staying in the conversation when you want to run. And it's about listening, even when it's very hard.

Repair is presence over perfection. Love over ego. It's what says, "This relationship matters more than being right."

Repairs don't just belong in big conflicts. They're just as powerful in small moments: the sigh, the shrug, the missed "thank you." Those little slips create quiet distance, and repair is how you close the gap.

You'll mess up sometimes. You'll say things you regret. But love gives you the courage to circle back. To ask, "How did that feel for you?" To say, "That wasn't my intention, and I want to understand." Love turns breakdowns into breakthroughs.

To repair well, start with awareness. Notice when there's a shift in tone, body language, or energy. That awkward silence or emotional pullback is an invitation—not to ignore, but to lean in.

Second, timing matters. Don't jump into repair mid-argument. Let the heat settle. Reconnect from a more grounded place.

Third, clarify your intention. Go in with the goal of understanding, not winning. Ask yourself: "Am I trying to fix this, or prove a point?" Let love be your compass.

And when you begin the repair, listen deeply. Reflect what you've heard. Speak in "I" statements. Own your experience without blaming theirs. Stay open, especially when feedback stings. That's not punishment; that's an opportunity to grow.

Most importantly, follow through. Check in later. Ask, "How are we doing?" Show them this isn't a quick patch-up. It's a commitment to connection. You won't always get it right. But you can always return with love. Because love doesn't promise perfect communication. It promises that no matter how messy things get, you can always find your way back.

When love leads, you don't shut down. You lean in. You don't pretend to be perfect. You show up real. You don't build walls; you build bridges.

That's how you own your love. That's how you own your healing.

So, take a deep breath, open your heart, and speak with intention. Whether it's a whisper, a belly laugh, or an "I'm sorry," let love shape your voice.

Because the most powerful conversations you'll ever have are the ones where love was the loudest voice in the room.

If you haven't gotten your Grace in Action Workbook, now is a great time to pause and get it so you can go deeper on what you've just learned and put the concepts... into action!

Go to gracesoulutions.com/workbook. You're welcome to also grab a journal you have and write your responses to the prompts that follow.

Grace Notes

Mini Journal Prompts:

1. Think about a time when love transformed a tough conversation. What helped shift the energy?

2. How do you naturally express love in communication and how do you receive it best?

3. What's one small way you can practice repair today with yourself or someone else?

Soul Notes:

Think of a moment when a conversation broke down.

What did you need at that moment, and what did they need?

Write about how love could have guided you back to each other, even if the words came out messy.

Love doesn't promise perfect communication. It promises that no matter how messy things get, you can always find your way back.

Chapter 11

Learning to Repair: Turning Breakdowns Into Breakthroughs

How to Heal with Intention, Not Just Words

Turning communication breakdowns into breakthroughs requires calling out the elephant in the room. If something feels off, it's because it is off. Ignoring the tension doesn't make it disappear. It only allows it to grow. Avoiding the issue doesn't heal it; it deepens the disconnect.

Instead of bottling up your feelings or pretending everything is fine, use your voice to create clarity and connection. You might say something like, "I feel like something's off between us. Can we talk about it?" or, "I didn't like how our last conversation ended. Let's check in." Naming what's present isn't about confrontation. It's about care. It's a courageous act of communication that says, '*I value this relationship enough to not let silence widen the gap.*' This is resilience in motion: choosing presence over avoidance, truth over tension.

Every time you do, you reinforce your confidence, not because you always know exactly what to say, but because you're willing to face discomfort with grace and integrity.

Calling out the elephant in the room isn't about confrontation; it's about connection. It's a courageous act of clarity that says, '*I care enough to not let this linger.*' This is part of using that resilience muscle you've been learning to build in reading this book. Choosing presence over avoidance, truth over tension. And each time you do, you reinforce your confidence. Confidence isn't just about saying the right thing; it's about having the courage to face what's uncomfortable and trusting that you can handle it with grace.

You're not perfect. No one is. And when communication breaks down, it's rarely just one person's fault. If you were reactive, distracted, or dismissive, take responsibility. This doesn't mean accepting blame for everything. It means owning your part with humility. Saying something like, "I reacted too quickly, and I realize I wasn't really listening," or "I should've handled that better, my bad," goes a long way.

Accountability signals growth. It shows the other person that you're not here to win; you're here to understand, reconnect, and move forward together.

When emotions run high, empathy can be your superpower. People don't just want to be heard. They want to feel understood. Empathy is the bridge between intention and impact. Instead of saying, "Well, that's not what I meant," you can offer, "I can see why that upset you, and that wasn't my intention." Instead of dismissing their feelings with, "You're overreacting," you might say, "I didn't realize how that came across. Let's talk about it." Empathy doesn't require you to agree with everything, but it does require that you respect the other person's experience. When you show someone that their feelings matter to you, defenses drop and the path to healing opens.

Repair is not a solo act. It's a shared experience built on mutual commitment to connection. If you go into the conversation trying to prove a point or declare who's right, you've missed the point of repair. Instead of pointing fingers, shift the energy to collaboration. Ask questions like, "How can we make sure this doesn't happen again?" or "What do you need from me moving forward?" These simple shifts show that you're invested not just in solving the problem, but in strengthening the relationship. When repair becomes a "we" thing, healing deepens.

One conversation won't fix everything. Repair is a process that unfolds over time. Following up shows you mean what you said. A thoughtful check-in, whether verbal or non-verbal, says, "I'm still here. I still care." That might be as simple as asking, "How are we doing?" or sharing a small act of kindness that reflects emotional follow-through. Trust isn't built in grand declarations. It's built in *consistency*. The way you show up after the apology matters just as much, if not more, than the words you said during it.

Everyone has a different communication style, and learning to navigate them helps make repairs smoother. If you don't take time to understand those differences, your communication styles will clash and connection will crumble. The example I shared earlier about myself and my husband perfectly illustrates this. I tend to be a Nurturer: detailed, structured, and eager to help. My husband, Norman, is a Humorous Communicator. He lightens tension through jokes and playfulness. That day with the Devil horn drawing? It was a moment where our styles collided. But because I understood his intention, I could laugh, recalibrate, and connect.

Here are the most common communication styles to be aware of. These categories are based on my own observations and experiences, drawn from years of working with individuals and couples navigating the energy of communication. Not everyone fits neatly into one category. Many people flow between two or three.

Fireballs are bold, passionate, and direct. They bring energy and determination to the conversation. But if they're unaware of their intensity, they can overwhelm others. If you're talking with a Fireball, be clear, concise, and grounded. Offer direct responses, but also invite pauses so they can slow down and listen.

Nurturers are caring, empathetic, and supportive. They naturally want to help and create harmony. Their challenge? They can smother or overextend themselves. When talking to a Nurturer, reassure them that it's safe to voice their needs too. Let them know disagreement doesn't mean disconnection.

Diplomats are the peacekeepers. They strive to see every side and value harmony, often acting as the bridge in difficult conversations. Their strength is their perspective, but because they are so open to different viewpoints, they may come across as indecisive or unsure of where they stand. To connect with a Diplomat, create an emotionally safe space that invites them to share their thoughts honestly and without judgment. Encourage them to trust that their voice matters, even when it may challenge the status quo.

Humorous Communicators, like Norman, use levity to defuse tension. Their lightness can lift a heavy conversation, but it can also feel dismissive if not timed right. With them, laughter is part of the process, but make sure the serious moments are also honored.

Miscommunication often happens not because of what's said, but because of how it's said. Style clashes are energetic mismatches, not personal attacks. Once you identify someone's communication style, you can adjust with intention instead of irritation. Meet Fireballs with clarity. Meet Nurturers with warmth. Meet Diplomats with calm. Meet Humorous Communicators with presence and timing. You don't need to change who you are. You just need to know how to meet people in the middle. When you do, repair becomes less about fixing something broken, and more about deepening mutual understanding.

No relationship is immune to miscommunication. People misread each other. People react before thinking. People get caught in their own heads. That's not failure. That's being human. But you know what strong communicators do?

They don't avoid conflict. They don't pretend everything's fine. They lean in, lead with love, and repair with intention. The true strength of communication isn't found in avoiding breakdowns, it's found in knowing how to mend them with grace.

And now that you've learned the heart of repair, it's time to put love into action. Let's explore what it means to practice love every day, in every conversation, with every word you choose.

If you haven't gotten your Grace in Action Workbook, now is a great time to pause and get it so you can go deeper on what you've just learned and put the concepts... into action!

Go to gracesoulutions.com/workbook. You're welcome to also grab a journal you have and write your responses to the prompts that follow.

Grace Notes

Mini Journal Prompts:

1. What communication style(s) do you most identify with—Fireball, Nurturer, Diplomat, or Humorous Communicator?

2. How does your style help or hinder you during repair conversations?

3. What is one adjustment you could make to support smoother repairs with others?

Soul Notes:

Is there someone in your life with whom you need to follow up after a difficult conversation?

What's one small action—verbal or non-verbal—that would show them you care and are committed to the connection?

One conversation won't fix everything. Repair is a process that unfolds over time.

Chapter 12

Love as a Lifelong Practice

Love + Communication = Growth

When you lead with love and learn to repair with confidence, you don't just become a better communicator, you become someone people feel safe with. That's powerful, because communication isn't just about clarity. It's about connection. Love is what gives your words depth, meaning, and impact.

This chapter is about growing into the kind of communicator who doesn't just speak well, but listens deeply, owns their part, and shows up with presence even when conversations might get uncomfortable. Because at the heart of every strong relationship and confident communicator is one simple truth: love is a practice.

It's in the way you listen. It's in the way you own your mistakes. It's in the way you show up, even when it's hard. Love isn't about being perfect; it's about being present.

Love is not just an emotion; it's a lifestyle. It's the way you show up in conversations, how you hold space for yourself and others, and how you choose to repair and reconnect when communication gets bumpy.

Love isn't passive. It's an active, daily commitment: a practice of patience, humility, and continuous learning. When you treat love as a practice rather than just a feeling, it transforms your relationships and your confidence.

I once met an older couple, Don and Nora, who had been married for over 50 years. They weren't the picture-perfect Instagram couple. They were the real deal, the kind who had weathered storms, raised kids, fought hard, and loved harder.

At a dinner party, someone asked them their secret. Don smiled and said, "We learned how to fight... and how to fix it." Nora added, "And we learned to love each other differently over time. Love now isn't what it was when we were 25. It's deeper, quieter, and more intentional."

What struck me the most wasn't their grand gestures or their longevity. It was the *small daily things.* The way Don instinctively pulled out Nora's chair. The way Nora touched his hand when he got quiet. The way they took pauses in their conversations, not to interrupt, but to give the other space.

They weren't afraid to admit when something didn't land right. They didn't avoid hard talks but they approached them with softness. They both said that what saved their relationship many times over wasn't romance. It was repair. *They practiced love like it was a lifelong language.*

Compare that to a woman I once worked with, Jasmine, who came to me feeling frustrated that every conversation with her partner turned into a standoff. She had grown up in a household where emotions weren't expressed. Where "love" was a feeling you assumed, not something you practiced. Learning to pause before reacting, to speak from vulnerability instead of control, and to listen without jumping to conclusions? That was new to her. It was uncomfortable at first. But the more she practiced, the more confident and connected she became.

She told me one day, "I used to think love was something you feel. Now I know it's something you do."

That's the power of love as a practice. Whether you've been doing it for decades or are just learning how, it's not about perfection; it's about presence, patience, and a willingness to keep showing up with your whole heart.

How do you actually practice love? That's quite a huge concept! Since we're all from different backgrounds and have different beliefs, it can show up in various ways. There are ways, though, that you can start to practice and make this a way of life.

Start by writing love letters to yourself. It may sound and feel awkward or a little strange. It may make you feel uncomfortable. But it's important to remind yourself how amazing you are, and to rewrite the message you've been telling yourself. You write a note, text, or tell a friend how amazing they are. Why do you forget to remind yourself of the same?

You can start by writing short notes or love letters to yourself. Leave yourself a Post-it note on your laptop or a note taped to your bathroom mirror. Make them short to start with, things like: *You handled that tough conversation with grace today. You're worthy of love and connection, no matter what. You matter. Period.*

Once you've started showing yourself love through words, extend that same energy outward. Think about the people who show up for you, the ones who cross your mind at random, or someone you haven't spoken to in a while. A simple message can shift someone's entire day.

It doesn't have to be long or dramatic. Send a quick text to say, "Thinking of you." Leave a sticky note on the fridge that says, "Thanks for always having my back." Or take a moment to write a heartfelt email to someone who's made a difference in your life. You never know how deeply your words might land. Even the smallest gesture of appreciation can create ripples of love, connection, and trust that last far beyond the moment.

We often think of love languages as physical touch, quality time, words of affirmation, acts of service, or receiving gifts. And yes, those matter. But mindfulness is a love language too. It's the quiet, steady kind of love that shows up in how present you are with yourself and others.

Mindfulness in communication means pausing before you speak, taking a breath to truly listen, and choosing your response with care. It can look like breathing through a tense moment instead of snapping back, or imagining warm, healing energy surrounding someone you love when words feel too heavy. It's those silent, intentional moments that say, '*I'm here. I'm grounded. And I'm listening.*' Mindfulness helps you respond, not react. That presence is one of the most powerful expressions of love there is.

Kindness isn't just something you extend to others. It's something you owe to yourself, too. It's easy to be hard on yourself when you stumble, to expect more, to beat yourself up over what you should have said or done.

But love begins with grace. And grace begins with kindness.

Be kind when you mess up, and remind yourself that mistakes are part of growth. Be kind enough to ask for help when you're overwhelmed or uncertain. And be kind to others, even in hard conversations, especially when emotions are running high. Leading with kindness doesn't mean avoiding the truth. It means delivering it with compassion.

Practice Love

Love isn't just reserved for big, emotional conversations or grand romantic gestures. It's in the everyday moments. It's in how you greet yourself in the mirror each morning, how you respond when someone interrupts you, and how you hold space for someone who's having a tough day. These moments may seem small, but they're where the practice of love truly lives.

The energy you bring into the room, the pauses you take, the tone you use, and the care behind your words all shape the experience of love for you and those around you.

Practicing love through communication means becoming more intentional with your presence. It's choosing to breathe before reacting, to speak with compassion even when you're frustrated, and to listen with the same level of attention you wish to receive. The more you practice love in the little things, the more natural it becomes when bigger challenges arise.

You don't have to wait for a crisis to communicate with love. You can start right here, *right now*, by building habits that align your words, your energy, and your intentions with care.

If you want love to flow naturally in your conversations, you have to practice it consistently, especially in the moments that seem too small

119

to matter. That's where your habits are formed. That's where the tone of your communication is shaped. These exercises are designed to help you embody love as a living, breathing practice—not just during tough talks or emotional moments, but in the simple, everyday interactions that often go unnoticed.

When you commit to showing up with warmth, patience, and presence in your daily communication, you don't just improve your relationships. You shift your entire energy. You begin to anchor your words in compassion, respond instead of react, and create safe spaces where connections can thrive. These aren't grand gestures. They're micro-moments that lead to macro shifts in how you love, listen, and lead with your voice.

Prioritize Quality Time—Without Distractions
You've read about prioritizing and being present several times in this book. Hopefully you can see the importance it plays in every facet of your life. Prioritize quality time by shutting off those distractions. Put your phone away, close the laptop, turn off the show you're binge watching.

Whether you're spending time alone or with loved ones, presence is the greatest gift.

Celebrate Yourself (Yes, You!)
You've probably cheered on a friend, sent a congratulatory text, or hyped someone up without a second thought. But when was the last time you did that for yourself? We're quick to recognize others, but slow to acknowledge our own wins.

It's time to change that.

Start making it a habit to celebrate even the smallest victories. You spoke up in a meeting? Celebrate that courage. You navigated a hard conversation with grace? That's growth worth honoring. You held a boundary without guilt? That's powerful. Celebration isn't about feeding your ego. It's about affirming your progress and reinforcing your confidence. You're growing, and that deserves to be seen, especially by you.

Speak Kindly To Yourself and Others

Words matter. Not just the ones you say to others, but the ones you whisper to yourself when no one else is listening. If you wouldn't say it to someone you love, it has no business being part of your precious inner dialogue.

Practice speaking kindly to yourself when you're frustrated, and to others when tensions rise. Replace harsh self-criticism with compassion. Shift blame into curiosity. Use your words to uplift, not to shrink. Whether you're offering encouragement or setting a boundary, let kindness guide your tone. Because the way you speak is the way you love. Every word you choose is a reflection of what you're practicing.

Choosing connection over correction, grace over guilt, and curiosity over criticism—that's what evolving through love and repair looks like.

It's also what a growth mindset sounds like. Heard of the growth mindset? It's that golden mentality that says, "I'm not here to be perfect. I'm here to grow, evolve, and improve with every conversation."

When you commit to learning from every miscommunication, every tough talk, every awkward moment, you turn setbacks into setups for something far greater.

Cultivating a growth mindset means shifting from self-doubt to self-belief. From asking "Can I really do this?" to "How can I grow through this?" It's the mindset that reminds you that your inevitable mistakes aren't failures. They're feedback.

Setbacks aren't signs to quit. They're invitations to stretch.

When you embrace a growth mindset, you stop playing small to stay safe and start stepping into conversations, opportunities, and challenges with curiosity and courage. You begin to trust that your voice, your story, and your perspective all matter—not when they're perfect, but when they're true. Growth doesn't come from trying to stay comfortable. It comes from choosing to show up anyway.

Cultivating a growth mindset looks like this:

1. Embrace Challenges—No More Playing It Safe
If you're avoiding difficult conversations because they make you uncomfortable, you're missing out on growth. Lean in. Get curious. Ask yourself, "What can I learn from this?" instead of "Why is this happening to me?"

2. Bounce Back Like a Boss
Not every conversation is going to be smooth. Some will flop. Some will sting. But instead of spiraling, reframe it. What went wrong? What would you do differently next time? Resilient communicators don't dwell; they adjust.

3. Celebrate Progress, Not Just Perfection
Stop waiting for the day when you'll magically have it all figured out. Progress happens in the small, daily moments when you choose love over ego, clarity over chaos, and connection over defensiveness. Give yourself credit for the work you're doing.

4. Tell Your Story, Own Your Lessons

People connect with stories, not with a mirage of perfection. Stop pretending you've got it all figured out! Share your wins, your lessons, and yes, your epic communication fails. Own your mistakes. Because when you do, you give others permission to learn and grow with you.

Misunderstandings? They're going to happen. Frustrations? Yep, those too. But resilient communicators don't crumble when things go sideways. They repair, rebuild, and come back stronger. And that, my friend, is the power of love in action.

Vulnerability? It's not a weakness. It's a courageous choice that invites intimacy and truth. It's what turns surface-level conversations into deep, soul-shaking connections. When you dare to be real, when you bring your full, unfiltered self into the conversation, you create space for others to do the same.

Here's your challenge: step boldly into love, own your voice, and embrace the messy, beautiful process of communication. Not because it's easy, but because it's so very worth it.

Because that's how we evolve through love and repair. Not by getting it 100% correct, but by showing up anyway. By staying present, staying open, and choosing connection, again and again.

Go out there, embrace love, and keep growing.

Because your words matter. Your connections matter. And most of all?

You matter.

If you haven't gotten your Grace in Action Workbook, now is a great time to pause and get it so you can go deeper on what you've just learned and put the concepts... into action!

Go to gracesoulutions.com/workbook. You're welcome to also grab a journal you have and write your responses to the prompts that follow.

Grace Notes

Mini Journal Prompts:

1. What does love as a practice look like in how I speak to myself and to others? *(Pay attention to your tone, words, and energy.)*

2. How can I respond with love the next time communication gets uncomfortable? *(Think pause, presence, and repair.)*

3. What's one small way I can show up today with more compassion, connection, or care? *(It could be for yourself or someone else.)*

Soul Notes:

Prioritize quality time without distractions. Make an effort.

1. How did it feel?
2. What happened?
3. What did you discover?

Growth doesn't come from staying comfortable. It comes from choosing to show up anyway.

Part 2

Living the Pearl of Grace™

What It Means to Be in GRACE.

You've heard the phrases: "Give yourself grace." "Have grace." "Thank God for grace." But what does "grace" really mean?

For me, grace isn't just a word. It's a way of being. It's my name, yes, but it's also my philosophy for life. Grace is about being grounded, authentic, and unapologetically YOU while also creating space for connection and compassion.

Grace isn't just something you receive. It's something you embody. It's already within you, supported by the Universe, by God (if that aligns with you), and by the people around you who reflect grace back at you.

Pearl of Grace isn't just a method; it's a movement. It's about showing up with confidence, clarity, and courage in your communication. It's about finding your voice, standing in your truth, and knowing how to repair when things may go sideways.

I was not always graceful in my communication. In fact, there was a time when my words were anything but kind, thoughtful, or intentional. One of the hardest, most defining moments of my life came after my mother-in-law passed away. My husband and I had a massive, emotionally charged argument that left deep wounds. I was miserable, hating my job, feeling trapped, and drowning in frustration. Instead of owning my emotions, I let them own me, and in that moment of anger, I hurled hurtful words at my husband, the kind that couldn't be unsaid.

I had unknowingly channeled my pain into words that echoed the very same hurtful phrases my own mother used on me. And then, the unthinkable happened. My husband, overwhelmed and broken, attempted to seriously harm himself.

That was my wake-up call. Everything stopped. The noise, the excuses, the justifications, all of it. I realized my words held power, and I had been wielding them recklessly, like a weapon instead of a bridge.

We sought counseling, not just to save our relationship, but to save ourselves. That was the moment my journey toward grace, groundedness, and gratitude truly began. Through counseling, mindset work, and deep reflection, I had to face a hard truth:

I was reacting instead of responding. I was projecting my own frustrations, wounds, and self-doubt onto the people I loved most. I blamed everything outside of me, my job, my environment, my circumstances, without taking responsibility for how I was showing up in my life and relationships. It was never about anyone else. Not my husband. Not my boss. Not my past. It was about me. My choices. My patterns. My lack of self-awareness.

The real work began when I stopped pointing fingers and started asking: '*What am I avoiding within myself? How am I contributing to my own unhappiness? What do I need to change, not in others, but in myself?*' Once I shifted my inner world, my outer world began to reflect that change.

I needed tools. Not just concepts, but actual, tangible tools to pull myself out of emotional chaos and into a space of grounded clarity. Tools such as meditation, breathwork, and journaling for self-reflection have been discussed throughout this book and woven into various practices for a reason. They work.

These are the tools I've personally found helpful for grounding myself, regulating my energy, and gaining clarity before, during, and after difficult conversations. Whether it's sitting in stillness, breathing with intention, or putting pen to paper to process your feelings and thoughts, these practices create space between your reaction and your response.

There are many different types of meditation, breathwork, energy work, and journaling approaches available. Explore what resonates with you. The goal isn't to do them perfectly, but to use them as supportive tools to help you stay centered, present, and in alignment with your truth.

Gratitude as My Cornerstone

If groundedness was my foundation, gratitude became the glue that held it all together. I stopped focusing on what was missing and started appreciating what was already here.

Acknowledging My Growth

Instead of beating myself up for past mistakes, I started acknowledging just how far I'd come. Every small step mattered, every moment of awareness, every time I chose understanding over reaction, every conscious breath before speaking.

Daily Gratitude Practice

At first, it felt forced, trying to write down things I was grateful for—when I felt anything but grateful. But over time, it became a joy. I started looking for tiny moments of appreciation throughout the day like the way my husband made me coffee in the morning, or how a friend checked in just to say hello.

Expressing Gratitude Out Loud

I stopped assuming people knew I appreciated them. Instead, I made it a point to say it. A quick text, a handwritten note, a heartfelt "Thank you for being in my life". These small acts of gratitude transformed my relationships.

Bringing Groundedness and Gratitude into Relationships

Today, my husband and I have a stronger relationship than ever before. Not because we never disagree (trust me, we do!), but because we've learned to navigate those moments with grace, respect, and gratitude.

Grounded Conversations

We've made a commitment to stay present when we talk. No phones. No distractions. If something triggers one of us, we pause instead of escalating.

Gratitude Rituals

We intentionally express appreciation for each other every week. Sometimes it's a simple "I loved how you supported me today." Other times, we share what we've learned from each other. This keeps our relationship nurtured and valued.

What exactly do I mean when I say live in GRACE?

Here's what each letter stands for and how it leads to a life of powerful, unshakable communication.

G – Gratitude

Grace begins with being grounded as discussed in the previous chapter by staying calm, present, and unshaken when life throws curveballs. But here's the secret weapon: Gratitude.

Gratitude isn't just about saying "Thank you." It's about focusing on what you have, rather than what you lack, and that shift in mindset?

It's a game-changer.

How Gratitude Changes Everything

Want better relationships? Say thank you more often.

Want more confidence? Appreciate what you've already accomplished.

Want more respect? Acknowledge the people around you.

Gratitude fuels confidence. Confidence fuels connection. Connection fuels powerful communication.

R – Reflection

Not every conversation will go perfectly. That's why reflection and resilience go hand in hand.

Reflection: The Secret to Better Communication

How do your words, tone, and energy affect others? Pay attention.

Are you listening or just waiting for your turn to speak? Be honest.

What patterns keep showing up in your conversations? Notice them.

Awareness is your greatest tool for reflection. When you reflect, you can course-correct, grow, and communicate with more impact.

A – Authenticity

When you speak from a place of authenticity, you're grounded in self-awareness, aligned with your worth, and confident in your voice. It's not about being loud or aggressive. It's about being honest, assertive, and aligned with who you really are. Authenticity is about showing up as your true self, without masks, without apology. It's the choice to drop the mask, own your truth, and communicate from a place of clarity and courage.

Authenticity – The Ultimate Confidence Booster

Drop the mask. The world needs the real you, not a watered-down version.

Your voice matters. When you stop people-pleasing, you start leading.

Not everyone will "get" you and that's okay. The right people will.

C – Connection & Compassion

Great communication isn't just about talking, it's about connecting. And connection happens when compassion is present, creating space for understanding, honesty, and trust.

Connection Is the Goal

At the heart of every meaningful relationship is connection. Compassion is what helps hold that connection together.

Give people grace. Nobody gets it right 100% of the time, but connection grows when we allow space for imperfection.

Put yourself in their shoes. Real connection starts with empathy and ask yourself, '*Would I feel safe or seen if I were spoken to this way?*'

Let go of the need to 'win.' The goal isn't to come out on top. It's to understand each other. Connection isn't built through control; it's built through care.

Compassion = Communication With Heart

Speak to yourself like someone you love. Self-compassion sets the tone for how you treat others.

You don't have to agree to be kind. Disagreement doesn't cancel out dignity.

Grace makes space. Compassion doesn't shrink the truth, it delivers it with care.

E – Energy & Empowerment

Energy speaks louder than words. Ever notice how some people light up a space, while others drain it? That's because of their energy. Energy fills the room before your words do.

How to Show Up with Empowering Energy

Confidence is contagious. Walk in like you belong there, because you do!

Your tone matters. *How* you say something matters as much as *what* you say.

Your body language speaks volumes. Open posture = open communication.

Empowerment = Owning Your Voice

Stop shrinking. If you have something to say, say it.

Use your voice for good. Speak up, not just for yourself, but for others.

Encourage others to shine. Empowerment is a ripple effect.

THE *PEARL OF GRACE* IN ACTION

This isn't just a philosophy, it's a way of life.

It's showing up in every conversation with confidence.

It's leading with love but holding your boundaries.

It's knowing when to speak and when to listen.

It's repairing relationships instead of running from conflict.

It's standing in your worth—unapologetically.

Grace isn't just something you receive. It's something you create. It's something you practice. It's something you own. And now, it's something you're ready to live.

Chapter 13

Gratitude:
Communicating with Grace

Lead with appreciation, speak with clarity, and build connection through grace.

If you've ever left a conversation feeling frustrated, drained, or unheard, it's likely because there was a lack of grace, either from yourself or the other person. Graceful communication is about being aware of how you show up in conversations, how you hold space for others, and how you ensure your voice is heard, without force or fear.

Gratitude sets the tone for everything that follows. When you approach communication with appreciation, whether it's for the conversation itself, the opportunity to listen, or even the potential challenge, you open the door to connection, not conflict. Living and communicating with grace starts by seeing the value in interactions, even when the conversation feels uncomfortable.

Gratitude in communication is not about being overly polite, or saying what someone wants to hear. It's about recognizing the value of every conversation, whether it's easy or difficult, whether you agree or disagree. When you express gratitude in communication, you create space for dialogue rather than debate; for appreciation rather than persuasion. It's about acknowledging each other's perspectives, not about proving who is right.

Let's explore four core qualities of gratitude in communication.

Clarity – Say what you mean, mean what you say, and let go of the need to sugarcoat or over-explain.

Compassion – Speak with kindness, even when the conversation is tough.

Patience – Give conversations room to breathe instead of rushing to fill the silence or force an outcome. Silence is not your enemy; not everything needs to be solved in the moment. Sometimes, the most graceful thing you can do is pause and allow space for reflection.

Respect – Respect does not mean backing down. It means honoring your viewpoint while also making space for someone else's viewpoint.

Clarity:
Clarity isn't just about choosing the right words; it's about choosing the right energy. Gratitude is the secret ingredient of clarity. When you lead with appreciation, you open the door to dialogue rather than debate and understanding rather than assumption. Clarity turns everyday interactions into meaningful exchanges, rooted in respect, connection, and mutual understanding.

You can infuse clarity into your conversations by acknowledging the other person's perspective, by showing you value what they're saying, even if you don't perhaps agree with what they are saying.

Compassion goes hand in hand with being present. Gratitude isn't just for when someone supports your viewpoint.

Instead of focusing on differences, ask yourself, '*What can I learn from other perspectives?*' If you are challenged, consider it a growth opportunity rather than an attack. Show that you value what they're saying, even if you don't agree. Instead of preparing your counterargument, actively listen and respond with understanding. Simple phrases such as, "Thank you for sharing your thoughts." "I appreciate your perspective," or, "That's an interesting way to look at it," can set a tone of respect.

Gratitude in communication is not about being overly polite or saying what someone wants to hear. It's about recognizing the value of *every* interaction or conversation, whether it's easy or difficult, whether you agree or disagree.

Clarity isn't about having all the right answers all the time. It's about showing up with appreciation and creating space for honest connection. That's where the magic of communication begins.

Compassion:
Grace in communication starts with compassion, both for others and for yourself. It's not just about speaking kindly to those around you, but also about how you respond to your own missteps. Compassion means letting go of the goal of perfection and offering yourself the same patience and care you give to others.

In conversations, compassion shows up as presence. It's choosing to listen fully instead of crafting a comeback, and responding with curiosity rather than criticism. Even if you disagree, you can honor the other person's perspective by saying things like, "I appreciate your point of view," or "That's a different lens to consider." These phrases signal respect and open the door to connection.

When you lead with compassion, you create a safe space for growth and mutual understanding. Focus less on being 'right', and more on learning. Ask, "What can I learn here?" Even challenging conversations become chances to deepen connection when compassion leads the way.

Stay grounded in curiosity. Show that you value the other person's experience, even if you don't share the same viewpoint. If you feel challenged, view it as an invitation to grow, not a reason to feel defensive.

Tools you can use to help you cultivate compassion are:

Challenge Negative Self-Talk: If your inner voice starts saying, '*I totally messed that up,*' or '*I should have said something different,*' stop and reframe. Ask yourself: '*Would I be this harsh to a friend?*' If not, change the narrative.

Prioritize Emotional Well-Being: Your emotional energy matters. Take care of yourself before and after important conversations so you can show up—fully present and confident. Whether it's deep breathing, a brisk or relaxed walk, or journaling, do what helps you stay balanced.

Establishing a Recovery Plan: No one masters communication overnight. It's an evolving process. Having a plan for recovery helps you regain your footing after a tough conversation and approach the next one with clarity and confidence.

Patience :
Patience is the space where real connection grows. In communication it is about giving conversations the space they need to breathe and unfold naturally. It's about resisting the urge to rush to conclusions, interrupt, or fix things immediately.

Patience allows deeper understandings to emerge because not every emotion, thought, or disagreement can be sorted out in a hurry. True connection grows when we allow people the time they need to express themselves fully, even if it's uncomfortable or takes longer than we expect. In the pauses, in the listening, in the willingness to wait, patience becomes a quiet form of love that strengthens communication.

How to Cultivate Patience in Communication:

Pause Before Responding: Take a moment before jumping in with your thoughts or reactions. Even a breath or a short pause can create space for better listening and more thoughtful replies.

Let Others Finish Their Thoughts: Resist the urge to interrupt or "fix" mid-sentence. Give the other person the respect of completing their point before you offer yours!

Normalize Silence: Not every gap in conversation needs to be filled immediately. Sometimes silence gives both people a chance to process, reflect, and respond with more clarity and care.

Respect :

Respect is the invisible thread that holds all healthy communication together. It is the foundation of safe conversation. It's about honoring another person's dignity, even when you disagree. Respect doesn't mean you have to agree with everything—or avoid speaking your truth. It means delivering your truth with care.

When you communicate with respect, you create emotional safety. You show others they are valued, even when perspectives differ. Respect keeps conversations open, courageous, and rooted in connection rather than control.

How to Practice Respect in Communication

Listen Without an Agenda: Don't listen just to counter-argue or "win." Listen to understand. Listening itself is a powerful act of respect.

Acknowledge Differences Without Dismissing: You can validate someone's feelings or experience without necessarily agreeing. Phrases like, "I can see why you'd feel that way," build bridges without sacrificing your own truth.

Use Empowering Language: Choose words that uplift rather than diminish. Speak to the best in others, even when navigating hard conversations, and you create a tone that invites a positive openness, rather than a negative defensiveness.

These four core qualities of gratitude sound simple in theory, but putting them into practice, especially during tense or emotional conversations, requires real awareness and intention.

Let me share a moment when choosing gratitude changed everything for me.

My Journey: How Gratitude Changed Everything

I wasn't always someone who communicated with intention. There was a time when my emotions took the lead. I reacted first and thought later. In those moments, my words sometimes cut deeper than I ever intended. It wasn't because I wanted to hurt anyone. It was because I didn't yet understand the power of gratitude, the gratitude for the person in front of me, the opportunity to speak, and the connection being built—even in really hard conversations.

Life, in its wisdom, gave me plenty of lessons in humility. I realized that real communication isn't just about getting your point across; it's about valuing the moment, valuing the relationship, and valuing the chance to grow. Gratitude shifted everything for me. It reminded me that every conversation, whether smooth or messy, is a real gift.

A chance to listen. A chance to understand. A chance to deepen trust.

Through mindfulness, journaling, and energy work, I started weaving gratitude into every part of how I communicate. I stopped seeing conversations as battles to win or lose, and started appreciating them as opportunities to connect. Gratitude softened my defensiveness. It replaced frustration with patience. It helped me listen not just to words, but to the heart behind them.

Today, gratitude is my default. I don't take communication for granted. I lead every interaction with appreciation, for the courage it takes to have honest conversations, for the people willing to show up, and for the ways we can all grow when we're willing to stay present. Gratitude didn't just change my communication. It changed my relationships, my confidence, and my heart.

My husband and I intentionally express appreciation for each other every week. Sometimes it's a simple "I loved how you supported me today." Other times, we share what we've learned from each other. This keeps our relationship nurtured and valued.

Grace in communication isn't just a skill. It's a way of being. It's the difference between reacting emotionally and responding intentionally. It's what allows you to speak your truth with confidence while creating space for others to do the same.

Gratitude shifts your energy, helping you see opportunities instead of conflicts, and collaboration instead of opposition.

When you integrate grace and gratitude into every interaction, your conversations will transform. People will listen to you differently. You'll walk away from discussions feeling confident, not drained. You'll build relationships rooted in respect, trust, and true connection instead of tension and miscommunication.

And the best part? You won't just be a better communicator. You'll become a more self-assured, empowered, and magnetic version of yourself; someone who leads with heart, speaks with clarity, and leaves every conversation better than you found it.

When you choose to bring grace and gratitude into your communication, you're not just changing the way you speak, you're changing the way you live. You create deeper trust, stronger bonds, and a sense of inner confidence that no one can take away. Conversations won't always be perfect, and people won't always respond the way you hope. But when you show up rooted in your truth, anchored in grace, and fueled by gratitude, you become a force for connection, healing, and positive change. And that's the kind of power that lasts far beyond the words themselves.

And never forget: your voice has power. Your truth deserves to be heard. And your grace will make an impact.

Now, go out there and communicate like the force of nature you were meant to be!

If you haven't gotten your Grace in Action Workbook, now is a great time to pause and get it so you can go deeper on what you've just learned and put the concepts... into action!

Go to gracesoulutions.com/workbook. You're welcome to also grab a journal you have and write your responses to the prompts that follow.

Grace Notes

Mini Journal Prompts:

Take some time to think about and reflect on recent conversations.

1. How do I typically show up in conversations? What does that say about what I believe about myself and others when I speak?

2. Where do I struggle most—with clarity, compassion, patience, or respect? What might be causing that, and how can I practice showing up differently?

3. How can I express gratitude in difficult conversations—without compromising my truth? What would I say differently if I led with appreciation?

Soul Notes:

Before your next important conversation—whether personal or professional—pause and write down three things you're grateful for:

- One about yourself
- One about the person you're speaking with
- One about the opportunity the conversation presents

Gratitude doesn't diminish your voice—it strengthens your presence.

Chapter 14

Reflect: Reframe with Grace

Shift Your Perspective, Strengthen Your Voice

Communication is not just about the words you say in the moment. It is also about how you grow, adapt, and evolve as a communicator. And that is where reflection and reframing come in.

Reflection allows you to take a step back, examine your conversations, and recognize what worked, what didn't, and where you can improve. Reframing helps you shift your mindset when communication challenges arise, ensuring that obstacles don't hold you back, but instead push you forward.

Together, these skills help you become a more resilient, confident, and adaptable communicator, someone who doesn't just speak, but leads conversations with clarity and intention.

Reflection is a mirror that shows you more than just how you communicate. It reveals who you are when you communicate. It's not about judgment or striving for perfection; it's about honest awareness.

Reflection shines a light on the patterns you repeat, the strengths you naturally embody, and the old habits that might still be holding you back. It's through practicing reflection that you stop operating on autopilot and start making intentional, empowered choices about the energy and impact you bring into every conversation.

As you reflect, you might begin to notice some key insights. You'll uncover your emotional triggers: those words, tones, or situations that make your heart race or your defenses rise. You'll see recurring patterns emerge. We all do.

Maybe you struggle to speak up when it matters most, or perhaps you tend to jump in and interrupt before someone finishes. Identifying these habits doesn't make you flawed—it gives you the power to shift them with intention and grace.

Reflection also reveals your communication strengths, the places where your natural gifts shine through. Maybe you're a trusted listener, the one people turn to for comfort or advice. Or you have a gift for seeing the heart of a situation quickly. Recognizing what you already do well allows you to lead with even more authenticity and confidence.

Some childhood moments fade quietly into the background. Others burn themselves into your memory, shaping the way you see trust, boundaries, and communication for many years to come. Here I will describe one of those moments, a defining experience that taught me about generosity, betrayal, and the unspoken power of words.

I was about eight or nine years old when my parents' friends came over for an overnight visit. They brought me a brand new toy, and I was beyond thrilled. I cherished my toys deeply; they weren't just playthings to me, they represented my father's hard work and the love and care that went into providing for our family. My father had a phrase he often said: "If you like something, you may have it." I understood it as a gesture of kindness, generosity, and abundance. But on that day, those words would take on a very different meaning.

The next afternoon, I came home from school, eager to dive back into my little world of toys. I ran to my toy box, only to stop cold. It was nearly empty. I blinked, thinking I must be imagining things. But the reality quickly settled in. Most of my toys were gone. The visiting adults had left that morning, and with my father's casual blessing, they had taken several of my cherished toys with them.

Without asking. Without a conversation. Without my consent.

I was devastated. To my eight-year-old heart, it felt like my entire world had been ripped apart. How could my parents allow this? Did they not care? How could something that was mine be given away without even a discussion? I cried for hours, overcome with heartbreak and confusion.

When my mother came home and saw the wreckage of my emotions, she didn't dismiss my feelings. She didn't tell me to "get over it" or shame me for being upset. She listened. She validated my pain, something I am deeply grateful for to this day. She also explained the situation to my father. That's when the real lesson landed, not just for me, but for him as well.

My father hadn't realized the unintended consequence of his well-meaning words. He meant to be generous, but what he should have said was, "You may choose one toy to take," not, "If you like something, you may have it." The damage, however, had already been done. And from that day forward, my understanding of trust and boundaries shifted.

Looking back now, I realize my attachment to those toys wasn't about material possessions. It was about value, respect, and the unspoken power of communication. What we cherish carries meaning far beyond the physical. Boundaries matter, even for children. And what's left unsaid can wound just as deeply as what is spoken.

That experience didn't just teach me about loss. It shaped the way I viewed generosity, trust, and ownership for years to come. I became hyper-aware of people taking things without asking. I became protective of what was mine. Without realizing it, one incident silently influenced how I interacted with others, well into adulthood.

Fast forward to college, when I crossed paths with the siblings of the family who had once taken my toys. The memory flashed instantly. I wanted to say something, to finally voice the hurt that had been tucked away inside me for years. But I held back. I didn't want to embarrass my parents. I didn't want to seem petty. And culturally, it felt inappropriate to rehash an old wound. Looking back, I now understand that if I had known the power of reflection and reframing, I could have honored my truth without bitterness. I could have said something like, "You know, I have a funny memory about when your family visited... let me tell you a story about how one moment changed the way I understood boundaries forever."

Instead, I swallowed it down again, protecting others at the cost of silencing myself.

Here's what I know now: Reframing isn't about forgetting or minimizing what hurt you. It's about transforming the story you tell yourself about what happened. It's about learning to protect yourself

150

with healthy boundaries, to speak your truth without apology, and to move forward without dragging old wounds behind you.

Reflection gives you insight. Reframing gives you the power. Together, they refresh your spirit and strengthen your voice, so you can communicate not from your old wounds, but from your hard-earned wisdom.

The beauty of reflection is that it puts you firmly in the driver's seat of your communication growth. Instead of waiting for outside validation or feeling stuck in old patterns, you gain the power to recognize, adjust, and evolve. Reflection isn't about finding what's wrong—it's about discovering what's possible. It's the secret to transforming not just how you communicate, but how you connect, lead, and live.

Reflection helps you see where you've been. Reframing enables you to step into where you're going, stronger, wiser, and more confident than before. To truly grow as a communicator, you must be willing to look back not with judgment, but with compassion and a willingness to evolve.

Reflection isn't about "obsessing over the past". It's about gathering insight that makes you more self-aware and intentional in your communication. It's the difference between saying, "That conversation was a disaster," and asking, "What can I learn from that conversation so I can do better next time?" Reflection gives you the space to recognize where your communication aligned with your values and where it missed the mark, without spiraling into self-criticism. Instead of replaying moments with regret, you begin to view each one as a stepping stone toward better clarity, connection, and confidence.

Reflection is like your personal communication audit. It helps you break down interactions, pinpoint strengths and areas for growth, and refine the way you express yourself.

When you take the time to reflect on your conversations, start by analyzing your interactions. Ask: What were the main points of the conversation? How did both parties react, not just verbally, but through body language, tone, and energy? Did your message come across the way you intended, or did it get lost in translation?

Taking a few moments to replay and study the interaction can reveal where alignment happened and perhaps where it slipped.

Next, focus on spotting your strengths and weaknesses. Reflection isn't just about finding what went wrong. It's about recognizing what went right! What communication habits serve you well? Maybe you're great at making people feel comfortable, or maybe you're skilled at keeping conversations focused and productive.

On the flip side, where do you tend to struggle? Maybe nerves cause you to over-explain, or maybe defensiveness creeps in when you feel challenged. Seeing these patterns clearly gives you the power to build on your strengths while consciously addressing the areas where growth is needed.

Finally, dive into understanding your emotional responses. Were there moments you felt frustrated, unheard, or misunderstood? What emotions surfaced, and how did you handle them in the moment? Paying attention to your emotional reactions is key to becoming a more grounded communicator. Emotions aren't the enemy. They're information. When you know what triggers you and how you typically respond, you can prepare yourself to stay centered, calm, and intentional even in the most challenging conversations.

The more you reflect, the more you learn about your communication tendencies, and the more empowered you become to refine your approach. Reflection turns experiences into growth, reactions into responses, and ordinary conversations into powerful opportunities for connection and understanding.

Make Reflection a Habit

Reflection is most powerful when it becomes a habit. Small, consistent efforts lead to significant breakthroughs over time. Here are ways to make reflection part of your routine:

Reflect on Your Conversations

Every conversation, good or bad, teaches you something. When you reflect and reframe, you become better at spotting patterns, adjusting your approach, and strengthening your communication muscles. It does not have to be a burdensome obsession, to review your interactions. Do it lightly and notice the main feelings and thoughts that arise.

At the end of each day, take a few moments to think about one conversation that stood out to you. Ask yourself: '*What worked? What didn't? What could I do differently next time?*' Reflecting while the interaction is still fresh helps you catch important details, things you might otherwise overlook, and allows you to build awareness of your communication habits in real time. Even one intentional reflection a day can create powerful momentum for growth.

Growth takes time. Give yourself permission to evolve at your own pace and embrace communication as a skill you refine over time.

Reflect with a Communication Journal

Writing things down brings clarity. Start keeping a communication journal where you jot quick notes about key interactions throughout your week. Reflect on how you felt during conversations, what you learned about yourself, and how you showed up. Prompts like, "How did I show up in this conversation?" or "What did I learn about myself today?" help you deepen your understanding of your communication style without getting stuck in overthinking. Your journal becomes a map of your evolution, something you can look back on to see how far you've come.

Seek Honest Feedback

Seeking feedback can feel overwhelming or even a little scary at first, but it's one of the most valuable tools for growth. Ground yourself in emotional regulation techniques, and approach feedback not as criticism, but as an opportunity to expand your awareness. Choose someone you trust, a friend, mentor, or colleague, and ask for their honest perspective.

Simple questions like...

- "Do you feel heard when we talk?" or
- "What's one thing I could improve in the way I communicate?"

...can open the door to insights you might not see on your own. Growth happens when you approach communication with curiosity, openness, and a willingness to evolve, not to some kind of standard of perfection, but to lifelong progress.

Practice Active Reflection and Reframe

Set aside a few minutes each week for deeper reflection on your communication journey. Look for recurring patterns, both positive and negative. Notice which situations bring out your best communication skills and which ones tend to trigger old habits. Active reflection isn't about criticizing yourself. It's about observing with curiosity and identifying small, powerful adjustments you can make.

Over time, these small shifts lead to major transformations in how you connect and express yourself.

Life Application

Real communication growth happens outside of a safe space. It happens when you're tired, frustrated, or feeling misunderstood, and you still choose to show up with grace. Reflecting and reframing isn't always easy. It's the harder work behind the scenes, the daily choice to pause, rethink, and re-approach conversations with intention rather than reaction. It's the work of rebuilding trust with yourself first, so you can show up powerfully with others.

Reflection keeps you humble. Reframing keeps you moving forward. Together, they form the foundation of communication resilience, the kind that strengthens every relationship you touch, including the one you have with yourself.

The world doesn't need perfect communicators—it needs brave ones. Communicators who are willing to reflect, reframe, and return to conversations with a little more grace, courage, and heart each time.

If you haven't gotten your Grace in Action Workbook, now is a great time to pause and get it so you can go deeper on what you've just learned and put the concepts... into action!

Go to gracesoulutions.com/workbook. You're welcome to also grab a journal you have and write your responses to the prompts that follow.

Grace Notes

Mini Journal Prompts:

1. What conversation today made me feel most proud of how I showed up? *(What did I do that reflected growth, grace, or courage?)*

2. What recurring pattern or trigger have I noticed in my communication lately? *(How could I reframe my reaction to create a different outcome next time?)*

3. When was the last time I held back my voice to protect someone else's comfort? *(What would it feel like to honor my truth next time with kindness and clarity?)*

Soul Notes:

Reflect back to a moment in your past, like I did in this chapter, that defined your way of thinking.

Replay it, and write down what you felt and how it framed your way of thinking about yourself.

Then, reframe the experience: what did that moment teach you about your values, your needs, or your growth as a communicator?

Emotions aren't the enemy.
They're information.

Chapter 15

Authentic: Communicating with Courage

Polish Your Pearl, Speak Your Truth

Authenticity means owning *all* of you, flaws and all. It isn't just about the words that come out of your mouth; it's about standing in every part of who you are without apology. For the longest time, I felt like I had to shrink, soften, and sanitize myself just to fit into certain spaces. I was taught to be polite, agreeable, and accommodating. But the day I stopped trying to be the palatable version of myself, the day I embraced my humor, my boldness, and my quirks, everything changed.

My confidence skyrocketed. My communication transformed. And most importantly? I felt free.

Authentic communication isn't about saying everything *perfectly*. It's about saying what's true. It's about showing up fully, without the masks, without second-guessing, and without shrinking to make others comfortable. Communicating with courage means standing firmly in your truth even when it feels uncomfortable, even when your voice shakes, and even when you aren't sure how it will be received. Authenticity demands that you bring all of yourself to the conversation: your values, your experiences, your heart, without editing yourself for acceptance.

When you speak authentically, you aren't just sharing information. You're building connections. True authenticity risks rejection and misunderstanding, but it also invites deep trust, respect, and relationships that are real—not manufactured. The fake personas we build to "fit in" eventually crack under pressure. People can feel when you're "performing" versus when you're real. When you're authentic, people trust you. They respect you. They feel drawn to you.

Authenticity creates deeper relationships with friends, partners, clients, and colleagues because it shows that you trust yourself enough to be seen.

Authenticity changes everything. It turns communication into something magnetic, fearless, and transformative. It helps you express yourself with clarity, confidence, and heart, no matter the audience, the situation, or the stakes.

So how do you strengthen it?

Start with self-reflection. You've already grounded your energy and become more present. Now ask yourself: '*What do I truly believe in? What do I stand for?*' The clearer you are about your core values, the easier it becomes to communicate from a place of authenticity. When you know your truth, you stop chasing approval. You speak with a grounded certainty that others can feel. Your values are the compass that guide your words, your choices, and the energy you bring into every conversation.

Embrace vulnerability. You've practiced managing your energy and opening space for deeper listening. Now it's time to drop the perfection act. Real connection happens when you're willing to be seen, flaws and all. Sometimes authenticity sounds like, "I don't know," or, "I need help," or, "I made a mistake." Vulnerability isn't weakness; it's the boldest act of truth-telling you can offer. When you let people see your real self, you invite deeper trust, richer relationships, and conversations that matter.

Listen *more* than you speak. Authentic communication isn't just about delivering your message. It's about truly hearing what's being shared with you. Listen without waiting to respond. Listen without assuming you already know. Listening more than you speak shows humility, respect, and emotional intelligence. It's a reminder that authentic connection is a two-way street, and your presence matters just as much as your words.

Let go of people-pleasing. You've built emotional resilience and practiced reflecting without judgment. Now it's time to let go of the need to make everyone happy. Authenticity means staying rooted in your truth, even when others don't understand or agree. It's about honoring your voice without shrinking, overexplaining, or apologizing for existing.

You are not responsible for managing everyone else's emotions. You are responsible for speaking your truth with clarity, kindness, and courage.

Confident communication comes from self-trust. When you communicate from a center of self-trust, you no longer feel the need to hold back or seek constant approval. You stand in your truth with quiet confidence. And in doing so, you naturally build greater respect in your relationships. When you are clear, direct, and authentic, people respect you more, even if they don't always necessarily agree with you. That's how you polish your pearl until it shines, strong and luminous from within.

Creative expression helps keep your authenticity alive. Whether it's through writing, art, music, storytelling, or another outlet, creative expression keeps you connected to your authentic self. It's where your soul gets to breathe and your truth gets to dance outside of conversation.

Creativity is not a luxury. It's a lifeline back to yourself. The more you express yourself creatively, the more natural it feels to show up, authentically, in your everyday communication.

Adding extra words to soften or over-explain your communication is not authentically you. It's a subtle way of apologizing for being yourself. The fear of seeming rude or too direct can cause you to pad your message with unnecessary apologies like, "I'm sorry but can you..." or, "I'm sorry, I have a question..." Over-explaining doesn't protect your relationships. It creates a facade that masks your truth. Over-apologizing and over-explaining are shields we create to avoid discomfort, but they also distance us from our real power. Authentic communication invites you to trust that your voice, as it is, is enough.

One of the biggest authenticity blockers I had to unlearn was over-explaining. For years, I felt like I had to justify my thoughts, feelings, and even my boundaries. I would start conversations with phrases like, "I'm sorry, I just think that maybe..." or, "I don't mean to be rude, but..." These habits might seem harmless, but they chip away at your authenticity. They send the message that you're unsure of your right to speak, or worse, that you need permission to exist.

I used to add layers of unnecessary words because deep down, I feared that being direct would be seen as being harsh. But assertiveness is not rudeness. Assertiveness is clarity. When you speak authentically, you don't need to beg, apologize, or soften your truth to be accepted. Over-explaining doesn't make you sound kinder. It makes you sound uncertain.

And uncertainty often invites misunderstanding and even disrespect.

The first shift was learning to say less and mean more. Instead of justifying everything, I began making clear, simple statements that honored my truth—without apology.

Example: Old me: "I can't make it because I have a lot going on, but I'll try to see if I can rearrange things..." Authentic me: "I won't be able to make it."

That's it. No apology. No backpedaling. Just truth, delivered with respect for myself and for the other person.

I also learned to embrace silence instead of rushing to fill every gap. Silence used to make me nervous. It felt like I needed to say more to earn acceptance. But now, I let my words land. I say what needs to be said and allow it to be enough. Authenticity sometimes means allowing the discomfort of silence to exist without scrambling to explain yourself out of it.

Finally, I replaced apologies with acknowledgments. If I make a mistake, I own it. If I have a question, I ask it without apologizing for taking up space.

Example: Old me: "I'm so sorry for asking this question..." Authentic me: "I appreciate your time. I have a question."

No apology necessary. Just clarity, confidence, and respect.

Stepping into your authentic voice isn't about being perfect or pleasing everyone. It's about trusting that who you are, and what you have to say, deserves space. It's about polishing the pearl that already lives inside you so your truth can shine through every conversation you have. Your voice doesn't need approval, but your truth does. When you own your authenticity, you own your power.

Speak it. Live it. Be it.

Have you ever said "Yes" to something when deep down you wanted to say "No"? Almost everyone has. But learning to say "No" clearly, confidently, and without apology is one of the most powerful ways to bring authenticity into your communication. When you say "No", you honor your boundaries. You stand rooted in self-trust, instead of fear or guilt.

Saying "No" doesn't make you selfish. It makes you real.

Saying "No" used to feel like breaking some unspoken rule, like I had to earn the right to set a boundary. I used to believe that unless I had a "good enough" excuse, I wasn't allowed to protect my time, energy, or peace. But here's the truth: you don't owe *anyone* an explanation for why you can't, won't, or *don't want to* do something.

Saying "No" is a complete sentence. Full stop.

The key to saying "No" with authenticity is to drop the excess fluff. Instead of piling on justifications, like "I would love to, but I'm really busy and I feel bad because I know it's important to you," you simply and kindly state your decision: "I won't be able to. Hope it goes well." No long-winded apologies. No guilt-tripping yourself into exhaustion.

You'll notice that people who are used to you always saying "Yes" might push back. That's normal. Stay grounded. If someone says, "Come on, just this one time?" you can simply respond, "I said no. Thanks for understanding." You don't need to defend, argue, or justify. Authentic communication respects both your boundaries, and theirs.

Finally, let go of the guilt. You are not responsible for managing other people's disappointment when you prioritize yourself. Setting a boundary with authenticity is an act of self-respect, and it teaches others how to respect you too. When you say "No" from a place of clarity and grace, you aren't rejecting others. You're choosing yourself.

And that's one of the most powerful expressions of authenticity there is.

While saying "No" with confidence is a personal act of authenticity, building relationships that support and celebrate your truth is just as essential.

You don't have to walk this path alone. In fact, you shouldn't. Authenticity thrives in spaces where you feel supported, challenged, and celebrated. Surround yourself with people who value truth, growth, and courageous communication.

Connect with like-minded individuals who understand the power of honest conversation. Whether it's a mastermind group, an online community, or a few trusted friends, build a circle that lifts you up, not one that pressures you to stay small.

Your environment matters, so choose one that feeds your authenticity, not your fear.

Engage in storytelling, not just the highlights reel, but the real, messy, beautiful truth. Share your journey, your struggles, your wins, your losses. When you speak your truth openly, you not only free yourself, you create a ripple effect that gives others permission to do the same.

Vulnerability strengthens community, and community strengthens courage.

The more you speak your truth, the more others will feel safe to speak theirs. Authenticity is not a destination, it's a daily decision. Keep choosing your truth, and your voice will never lead you wrong.

If you haven't gotten your Grace in Action Workbook, now is a great time to pause and get it so you can go deeper on what you've just learned and put the concepts... into action!

Go to gracesoulutions.com/workbook. You're welcome to also grab a journal you have and write your responses to the prompts that follow.

Grace Notes

Mini-Journal Prompts:

1. **Set Personal Goals:** Where do you want to improve? Do you want to be more direct? Less apologetic? More confident in stating your needs?

2. **Feedback Loops:** Ask for feedback—but only from people who genuinely want to see you grow.

3. **Embrace the Lessons of Mistakes:** Messing up isn't failure—it's education. What's one misstep that you can learn from?

Soul Notes:

Think of a time when you said "yes" to someone, and you really wanted to say "no". Taking what you learned in this chapter, how can you communicate with courage and authenticity?

Authentic communication isn't about saying everything perfectly. It's about saying what's true.

Chapter 16

Connected & Compassionate: Communicating with Presence

Kindness and Connection Transform Every Conversation

Connection in communication isn't just about exchanging information. It's about creating a space where people feel safe to be themselves. When you show up with presence, curiosity, and authenticity, you make others feel like they matter.

And that, my friend, is what turns a conversation from forgettable to life-changing.

No one likes talking to a brick wall. When you truly connect, you don't just make small talk; you create moments of trust, warmth, and deep understanding. When you lead with compassion, you invite openness, honesty, and "realness" into your conversations. Communication isn't just about exchanging words. It's about creating energy, building relationships, and making people feel seen, heard, and truly valued.

You've heard this before in this book: no one wants to pour their heart out to someone who's only half-listening, waiting for their turn to speak. When you combine connection with compassion, you elevate every interaction from meh to meaningful. That's where the magic happens.

Connection matters. It makes people feel valued. It turns surface-level chatter into soul-level conversations. But connection goes beyond that. It builds trust, rapport, and genuine relationships. It encourages people to open up, share, and be authentic.

You've felt that power. Ever walked away from a conversation feeling energized, lighter, and just plain good? That's connection. Some connections are loud and immediate. Others are like seeds, planted silently and blooming later in unexpected, beautiful ways.

Take my story, for example. My husband and I first crossed paths in 1994. I was a university student visiting Scotland with my friend, Karen. As we walked up the Royal Mile in Edinburgh, we passed a group of guys. One of them was my now-husband. Neither of us spoke. Neither of us knew this would be a moment to remember.

Five years later, I moved to Scotland and stayed at a hostel. As fate would have it, he was there. We started talking, and I casually mentioned my trip in '94. That's when he floored me—he remembered me! He remembered what I was wearing, my hairstyle, even my friend, Karen. Every. Little. Detail.

That moment completely blew my mind. It wasn't just coincidence. It was a quiet and profound connection that had been waiting to unfold. (I like to joke that I didn't just bring memories back from Scotland—I brought home the most expensive and priceless souvenir of all.)

Sometimes, connection isn't loud. It's a moment, a kind gesture, a presence that lingers. It's not just romance. It's life. Every time you make eye contact, hold a door, or share a smile, you might be planting a seed of connection that will bloom later.

Living in Scotland threw me into a world of communication differences I wasn't prepared for. I quickly learned that speaking the same language doesn't guarantee understanding or connection.

Like the vocabulary: Toppers = Boots (Not hats!) Jumper = Sweater (Not a gymnast!) Half Twelve = 12:30... or 11:30. (What even?!)

One of my favorite culture-shock moments? The bakery incident. I asked for "biscuits"—meaning cookies—and was met with confused stares. In Scotland, cookies are called biscuits, and what Americans call biscuits, they call scones. It was a deliciously awkward reminder that even when we speak the same language, we don't always mean the same thing. It made me realize that clarity in communication isn't just about words—it's about shared meaning. And sometimes, a little confusion can be the beginning of a connection.

Lesson learned: Words matter. And sometimes, they mean different things to different people.

Instead of getting frustrated, I leaned into compassion. I asked questions, laughed at myself, and embraced the differences. Compassion allowed me to connect.

To truly connect, you need compassion. Connection without compassion feels shallow. Compassion without connection feels distant. But when they come together, something magical happens. They make people feel safe, appreciated, and empowered to express themselves, whether it's a casual chat or a tough conversation.

How do you know when you're truly connecting with someone? Watch their body language. They'll relax. Their shoulders will drop. They stop nodding and start engaging. When people feel safe, they open up. It's no longer just about the weather.

Something else happens too. The energy shifts. A connected conversation feels alive, even in serious moments.

Compassionate communication isn't about fixing. It's about supporting. When people feel supported, they feel safe to open up. They feel heard, understood, and valued. Just like you want to feel truly listened to, others need that same space. Compassion builds trust, strengthens relationships, and transforms even the toughest conversations into opportunities for healing.

A few ways to practice compassionate communication:

- Instead of "That's not a big deal," try, "That must have been really tough for you."
- Pause and let the other person finish before responding.
- Ask with curiosity: "Can you tell me more about that?"
- Acknowledge emotions: "I can see why you'd feel that way."
- Offer presence: "I'm here for you."

Compassionate communication also means resisting the urge to assume. When you replace judgment with curiosity, you make space for understanding.

Assumptions block connection. Clarity builds it. When in doubt, ask. The more you practice curiosity instead of jumping to conclusions, the more your relationships and confidence flourish.

Go beyond small talk. Ask, "What's something exciting that´s happening in your life?" Be fully present. Turn off distractions. Listen to listen, not to reply. Put yourself in their shoes. Validate their feelings. Let go of the need to be right.

Some people are difficult to talk to. Their walls are high, their words are sharp, their energy guarded. But compassion can soften even the rockiest conversations. It doesn't mean necessarily agreeing. It means seeing the person behind the words and responding with grace. Compassion transforms conflict. It keeps you present when emotions run high. It helps you listen without becoming defensive, and to respond in ways that heal.

During conflict, try this:

- Make eye contact and show you're listening.
- Instead of "You're wrong," say "I see it differently. Let's talk."
- Take a breath before responding.
- Ask clarifying questions: "What specific statements or actions upset you?"
- Offer support: "That sounds tough. I'm here for you."
- Focus on solutions, not blame.

Compassion isn't weakness. It's wisdom. It's the courageous choice to prioritize connection, even during conflict. When you show up as a confident, compassionate communicator, things shift. You feel more grounded, powerful, and at peace. You stop shrinking, overthinking, or second-guessing. You stand tall in your truth.

You attract better relationships. You stop wasting energy on people who don't respect you. You build deeper, more meaningful connections with those who do. Your energy speaks louder than your words, and the right people will rise to meet it.

Conflict stops feeling like a warzone. You no longer dread difficult conversations. You walk in with calm clarity and a fearless fire. You know how to handle what comes gracefully, wisely, and without losing yourself.

You stop shrinking to make others comfortable. You stop swallowing your words. You speak up. You own your space and your voice without apology.

You walk away from conversations feeling empowered, not drained. No more emotional hangovers. No more replaying every word. You know that you spoke with clarity, intention, and heart. And that is powerful beyond measure.

The way you communicate determines the quality of your life.

When you master connection and compassion, your relationships thrive, your confidence soars, and your ability to navigate even life's messiest moments becomes unstoppable. This isn't just about talking. It's about feeling heard, valued, and fully expressed in your life.

It's about walking into every conversation knowing you don't have to prove yourself. You just have to be yourself. It's about owning your worth, standing firm in your truth, and bringing more kindness, courage, sass and badassery into the world.

Go ahead. Speak boldly. Love deeply. Communicate fearlessly.

Because when you do, everything changes.

If you haven't gotten your Grace in Action Workbook, now is a great time to pause and get it so you can go deeper on what you've just learned and put the concepts... into action!

Go to gracesoulutions.com/workbook. You're welcome to also grab a journal you have and write your responses to the prompts that follow.

Grace Notes

Mini Journal Prompts:

Pick one or reflect on all three after any meaningful interaction or at the end of your day:

1. Was I fully present and genuinely listening?
2. What subtle moment of connection stood out to me?
3. How did I show up with compassion today, even in a small way?

Soul Notes:

For the next week, reflect daily on how you intentionally created a deeper connection.

1. Where did you show up fully in a conversation today?
2. How did you practice compassion, even when it wasn't easy?
3. What changed when you prioritized connection over just exchanging words?

Compassion isn't weakness.
It's wisdom.

Chapter 17

Energized & Empowered: Communicating with Impact

Your Energy Speaks Louder Than Words

Communication without energy is like trying to dance without music. It falls flat, lacks rhythm, and doesn't move people the way it should. Energy is the invisible force behind every conversation, and whether you realize it or not, it's always speaking for you. Think about it. You can say, "I'm excited to be here," but if your tone is dull and your body language screams boredom, no one's buying it.

Your energy tells the truth, even when your words don't.

Empowerment, on the other hand, is what happens when you take control of that energy. It's about recognizing the power in your presence, using it intentionally, and ensuring your communication lands with impact, clarity, and confidence.

If you want to own your space in the room, influence and inspire, and ensure your message sticks, then you need to master the energy behind your communication. To my way of thinking, that is not a sales or marketing motivation, it is a motivation to add quality interactions to your community and ultimately help people to find peace and joy.

Every interaction is an exchange of energy. You've felt it before. When someone speaks with passion and conviction, you lean in. When someone drones on with low, lifeless energy, your brain checks out faster than on a bad date. Your energy is your *first* impression, your lasting impression, and everything in between. It can either elevate a conversation, making it engaging and dynamic, or drain it, leaving everyone disengaged.

You want your energy to work *for* you, not against you. One of the most powerful tools you have is your voice. Before any important conversation, do a quick "power voice" check:

Stand tall, take a deep breath, and speak with intention. Let your voice carry confidence.

Pace: Speaking too fast makes you sound nervous. Speaking too slowly makes you sound unsure. Find a rhythm that commands attention without overwhelming your listener. (Unless you're a New Yorker; then fast-talking is practically a love language! Just make sure people can still follow you!)

Intentional Pauses: Pausing strategically during conversations allows for reflection, helps emphasize essential points, and gives the other party time to process information.

Tone: A monotone voice kills engagement. Infuse variety, warmth, and conviction into your tone to keep people hooked.

Volume: Speak too softly, and your words lose impact. Speak too loudly, and you might overwhelm your audience. Own your voice with confidence.

Clarity: Slurring, mumbling, or trailing off weakens your message. Speak crisply and deliberately.

Your body is always talking. Even before you utter a word, your facial expressions, posture, and gestures set the tone for how your message is received. Non-verbal energy matters. Posture signals strength or uncertainty. Crossed arms and hunched shoulders can come off as closed-off and hesitant, while steady eye contact and a relaxed stance say you're grounded and open. Smiles? Inviting. Frowns or blank looks? Not so much.

Gestures should be purposeful, not fidgety or excessive. Intentional movement adds energy and emphasis. Fidgeting distracts. Record yourself speaking. Watch your body language. Is it supporting your message or working against it?

People don't just listen to your words; they *feel* them. Your emotional energy is contagious. If you're passionate, people feel it. If you're calm, they feel safe. If you're tense or defensive, they shut down. Your inner state leaks into every interaction. Before any conversation, ask yourself: '*What energy am I bringing? What energy do I want to bring? How do I want others to feel afterward?*' If your energy's off, reset. Breathe. Recenter.

Wandering into a conversation without intention is like driving without a destination. Are you here to inspire? Then bring passion. Are you here to resolve conflict? Then bring calm and clarity. Are you here to make an impact? Then bring confidence and conviction. Your intention sets your energetic tone. Before stepping into any interaction, define your intention: "I am here to connect." "I am here to lead." "I am here to listen with compassion."

Your energy speaks before you do, and it lingers long after the words are gone. When you align your verbal, non-verbal, emotional, and intentional energy, your communication becomes magnetic. People don't just hear you; they feel you. They trust you. They want to engage with you. This isn't about being "on" all the time. It's about being aware. It's about showing up in a way that matches your message and honors your purpose. When your voice, body, emotions, and intention work in harmony, you become a communicator who doesn't just deliver words; you create impact.

Before your next conversation, ground yourself; ask: '*What energy am I bringing into this room?*' Then lead with that energy on purpose. Because when your presence aligns with your purpose, your message lands exactly how you meant it to. And that's where real connection begins.

Energy is everything. It fuels your presence, drives your communication, and determines the impact of every conversation. The most empowered communicators don't just speak well. They manage their energy well. Not every space calls for high energy. Sometimes, toning it down is more effective than turning it up.

Reading the emotional temperature of a room before diving in is one of the most overlooked communication tools. If the energy feels tense, bring warmth. If it feels heavy, bring lightness. If it feels chaotic, slow it down. Matching and slightly elevating the room's energy builds trust and connection because it shows people you're tuned in, not just performing. Before diving into a conversation, take five seconds to read the environment. Match the energy first, then elevate it with calm confidence.

Your emotional energy sets the tone before a single word is spoken. If you're walking into a conversation feeling frazzled, irritated, anxious, or off-balance, that energy will leak through your body language, voice, and word choice. If you're not intentional, you might let your emotions lead the conversation instead of your message.

You don't have to "fake" positivity. You just have to choose not to let negativity run the show.

When you feel your energy slipping into frustration, fear, or defensiveness, pause and take a moment to recalibrate. Take a deep breath and drop your shoulders. Release the tension you're holding in your jaw, your fists, or your chest. Remind yourself why you're here, what you want to say, and how you want to show up. Then speak from that space. Let your words be guided by purpose, not pressure. When you lead with calm clarity, people lean in. They feel the shift. Before responding, ask yourself: '*Am I speaking from my grounded self or my triggered self?*' Pause, reset, and realign with your intention before you let words fly.

Not every conversation deserves unlimited access to your attention, energy, or emotional reserves. Some situations and people will try to pull you into drama, drain you with negativity, or leave you feeling energetically exhausted. Just because someone speaks doesn't mean you have to fully engage.

Protecting your energy starts with awareness. If someone comes at you with aggression or passive negativity, resist the urge to mirror it. Instead, remain grounded and neutral. Don't let their chaos become your state.

If the conversation begins to spiral into blame, complaining, or emotional dumping, you have the right to redirect or step away. This isn't avoidance; it's energetic responsibility. You are allowed to decide

183

when to stay, when to guide, and when to exit. For example, you can say, "I hear that this is hard. Can we revisit this later when I can give it the attention it deserves?" or "I need a break to reset my energy before continuing this conversation."

If it's not adding value, clarity, or connection, it might not be worth the energy you're investing. Ask yourself mid-conversation: Is this feeding my purpose or draining my peace? If it's the latter, pivot, pause, or gracefully exit.

Empowerment is the process of recognizing and embracing your inner strength, and it is intrinsically connected to the energy you bring to your communication. When you communicate with empowerment, you are confident in your ability to express your truth, assert your needs, and stand in your worth. Empowered communication stems from self-assurance. You believe in the validity of what you have to say and are willing to express it without fear. You're not looking for validation; you're validating your own strength.

When empowered, your communication is clear and succinct. This clarity allows others to understand your message quickly and fosters more productive conversations. When you're confused, your delivery reflects that confusion. When you're clear, so is your message, and others will understand it easily.

Empowered communicators respect not only their own needs, but also those of others. This mutual respect strengthens the bonds between communicators and fosters a collaborative environment. Respect yourself and others. As Aretha Franklin once sang, "*R-E-S-P-E-C-T, find out what it means to me!*"

Empowered individuals often take the initiative to share their thoughts, feelings, and needs without hesitation or apology. They create opportunities for dialogue rather than waiting for others to engage.

Understanding your worth is the foundation of empowerment. Reflect on your strengths, achievements, and what makes you unique. This self-awareness fosters a more confident communication style.

If you'd like a little extra support (hint, hint!), I've created a few tools to walk with you: the *YOU MATTER, Yes You Do* card deck, filled with journal prompts to help you explore your worth one question at a time; the *Liu (Loo) Loo Life's Wisdom In Every Flush deck*, for when you need some lighthearted but sassy wisdom to help you flush out what no longer serves; the *Grace in Action Workbook*, your space for deeper self-reflection and integration; and the *Grace Notes* card decks, designed to support your voice with clarity, compassion, and confident communication—no overexplaining required.

Set healthy boundaries. Empowerment involves knowing your boundaries and communicating them assertively. Taking care of your limits is self-care, not selfishness.

Challenge limiting beliefs. Replace negative self-talk with affirmations that reinforce your ability to communicate clearly and confidently. Welcome feedback as growth, not as a threat.

In today's beautifully diverse world, communication doesn´t mean taking a one-size-fits-all approach. What's considered empowered and energetic in one culture might be viewed as aggressive or inappropriate in another.

Your words matter—but so do your presence, your tone, and your ability to read the room through a cultural lens. If you want your energy to resonate across different backgrounds, cultural awareness is non-negotiable. It's not about watering down who you are. It's about meeting people where they are, so your message lands with respect and clarity.

When you communicate with cultural awareness, your energy becomes more inclusive. You create space for others to feel heard, seen, and respected, even when they communicate differently. You will become more effective. You avoid misunderstandings by understanding the nuances of different communication values. You build bridges instead of barriers. You become someone people trust to speak with both heart and awareness.

Energy looks different across cultures. What one culture sees as confidence, another might perceive as aggression. Being aware of these differences is essential to communicating with clarity, connection, and respect.

High-energy communicators often express themselves with enthusiasm, animated gestures, and vocal inflection. Think of Italian, Latin American, or Middle Eastern cultures, where passion is welcomed and seen as engaging. In contrast, low-energy communicators tend to prioritize calmness, pauses, and minimal movement. Think of Japanese, Scandinavian, or East Asian cultures, where restraint is a form of respect and listening carries great value.

If you're used to fast-paced, expressive dialogue and find yourself met with quiet nods or measured tones, don't assume the other person is disengaged. Their energy is simply calibrated differently. Communication is still happening—it just may be quieter, slower, and more deliberate.

Empowered communicators learn to tune in, not take it personally, and adjust with grace.

Empowered communication isn't about asserting yourself louder. It's about connecting more consciously. Let go of assumptions. Your way of communicating isn't universal; it's cultural. Direct eye contact may show confidence in some cultures but disrespect or aggression in others, such as Indigenous Australian culture. Be curious, not critical. Ask questions to better understand the rhythms and nuances of someone else's communication. Mirror and match respectfully. Adjusting your tone, pace, and presence isn't about abandoning your identity.. It's about honoring who they are.

As you move through the layers of energetic presence and cultural awareness, remember this: communication is a living, breathing relationship. The more attuned you are to your own energy and how it's received by others, the more empowered you become.

Empowerment is not just an individual pursuit. It grows stronger through collective intention. When we build communities that value clarity, empathy, and awareness, we create spaces where everyone can speak freely, be fully seen, and express themselves without fear.

Your voice is powerful. Your presence is magnetic. Your energy has an impact. Own it. Live it. Lead with it. When you master the energy behind your words, you don't just communicate. You create change. Across cultures. Across conversations. Across the world.

Communication with impact isn't about being loud, bold, or "perfect". It's about being intentional with your presence, aligned with your values, and aware of the energy you bring.

The more attuned you become to your voice, your body, and your environment, the more magnetic and meaningful your communication will be.

If you haven't gotten your Grace in Action Workbook, now is a great time to pause and get it so you can go deeper on what you've just learned and put the concepts... into action!

Go to gracesoulutions.com/workbook. You're welcome to also grab a journal you have and write your responses to the prompts that follow.

Grace Notes

Mini Journal Prompts:

1. How does my energy shift in different conversations? Think about recent interactions. Were you calm, rushed, enthusiastic, irritated? What energy did you bring into the space, and how do you think it was received?

2. What part of my communication needs more alignment: my words, my tone, or my presence? Explore where you might be saying one thing, but your body or emotional energy is signaling another.

3. What's my go-to reset when I'm not in the energy I want to bring? Whether it's breathwork, grounding, visualization, or silence, write out your go-to ritual. If you don't have one, this is the time to create one.

Soul Notes:

Before a conversation, ask yourself:

1. What's my emotional state right now?
2. What energy do I want to bring into this space?
3. How do I want the other person to feel after this conversation?

Go shine your pearl,
with grace.

Chapter 18

Living Your Journey Through the Pearl of Grace

Where Your Voice Meets Your Life

Communication is more than the words you say. It's the energy you bring, the presence you hold, and the impact you leave behind. The *Pearl of Grace* is about more than speaking your truth—it's about embodying your worth, communicating with purpose, and creating meaningful connections through both verbal and non-verbal expression.

As you have read throughout this book, and through your own life experiences, you know that actions always speak louder than words. When you align your communication with who you truly are, that's when you step into your power.

Growing up, I saw firsthand how words could hurt and how they could shape a person's self-worth. My mother, like many in traditional Asian households, had her own struggles with communication. In moments of frustration, she would say things that stung, words that could have broken me if I had let them.

One phrase she used, in particular, stands out: "When you get married, I hope your husband physically abuses you." Ouch.

I knew this wasn't really about me. It was simply the only way she knew to release her agitation. Her words were sharpened by her own upbringing and the culture she came from. In her mind, harshness built resilience. For me, those words became something else entirely: a guidepost for what I would *not* accept.

I had a choice. I could internalize those words, believe I was unworthy of kindness, and settle for mistreatment. Or I could break the cycle. I made a vow to choose relationships, romantic and otherwise, where words and actions aligned, where respect was the foundation, and where love was demonstrated and shown, not just spoken.

My grandmother, on the other hand, was a woman of quiet wisdom and sharp observation. She had seen enough in her lifetime to understand that words can be deceptive.

Her greatest advice?

"Never listen to what a man says; watch what he does." Those wise words from my grandmother saved me from a whole lot of unnecessary heartache.

My grandfather was a smooth talker. A master of grand gestures, on paper. He wrote my grandmother a love letter so beautiful that she agreed to marry him. Once the vows were exchanged, his words lost their meaning. His actions showed something else: stinginess, favoritism, and a complete disregard for my grandmother's emotional well-being.

One glaring example? His frugality. He had a knack for collecting things others no longer wanted. Some might call it scrappy or resourceful—he simply saw it as practical. Once, he brought home a used mattress left out on the curb, proudly declaring it "perfectly fine." He rarely believed in buying anything new if he could find something "good enough" elsewhere. To him, it was about saving money and making do.

He wasn't stingy only with others; he was frugal with himself, too. Perhaps it was a habit shaped by his upbringing or the times he lived through. Even so, to my grandmother, his penny-pinching ways often felt more like dismissiveness than thrift, especially when comfort and care were on the line.

She spent her marriage learning the hard way that words without actions mean nothing. And she passed that wisdom down to me, a lesson I would carry into every relationship in my life.

When I met my husband, I didn't just listen to his words. I watched. And what I saw was a man who didn't just say he cared, he proved it.

One defining moment came early in our relationship.

I had an important meeting in an unfamiliar town, and I was stressing out. I hated getting lost, I hated being late, and I was spiraling.

My husband had just finished an exhausting night shift as a nurse. He was running on fumes, and honestly, no one would have blamed him if he had said, "You'll be fine, just use a map." GPS wasn't invented at that time. But he didn't. He got up, freshened up, and drove me there himself. He sat in the car, sleep-deprived but unwavering, waiting for me to finish.

When I came out, he drove us home, cooked me dinner, and headed straight back to work that evening. No grand speech. No expectations. Just love in action.

The little things matter too. Shopping trips? He gives honest feedback on what looks good, not to control, but because he genuinely wants me to feel confident. Rough days? He shows up, no questions asked. Big dreams? He supports them with his actions, not just empty encouragement.

If you want to know how someone truly feels about you, don't just listen to what they say. Observe how they act. Non-verbal communication is more than "body language". It's the effort someone puts in, their consistency, their energy, and their willingness to show up when it matters most.

A strong relationship, romantic or otherwise, is built on presence. The kind that shows up even when it's inconvenient or uncomfortable. It's nurtured through small but meaningful gestures because love often lives in the details, not the grand declarations. And it's sustained through consistency because while words can inspire in the moment, it's repeated action that builds trust and keeps connection alive.

This goes both ways. I make sure my husband feels seen, heard, and supported too. Love isn't about grand declarations. It's in the everyday moments. Because at the end of the day, words might make promises, but actions prove them.

The *Pearl of Grace* isn't just about what you say. It's about who you are, how you show up, and how you align your words with your actions. It's about ensuring that your presence, your communication, and your energy create a ripple effect of confidence, connection, and compassion.

By now, you've done the work: read the words, grounded your energy, reflected in your journal, and shown up for yourself with intention. Take a moment to check in. Are your words aligned with your actions? Are you showing up in a way that reflects your values and truth? Are you communicating with care, clarity, and authenticity?

You don't need to start from scratch. You've already begun. Everything you've practiced so far has built a foundation of empowered, intentional communication. Keep building. Let your voice reflect your growth. Let your presence speak before you do.

Let your continued commitment to this work shape not just how you communicate, but how you live.

If my mother's words had shaped my beliefs, I might have missed out on the profound love and unwavering care my husband provided. Instead, I chose to rewrite the narrative. I chose to affirm my worth and recognize that love isn't about what people say, it's about what they do. My grandmother's wisdom became my guide. Because of it, I found myself watching for the actions that embody true care, respect, and compassion.

Before you confidently own your voice and presence, you have to discover your PEARL. That is your inner wisdom, your self-worth, and your unique brilliance. Once you recognize this, you can move with GRACE, showing up with alignment, authenticity, and intention in every conversation, relationship, and decision.

It's about showing up with integrity, knowing your worth, speaking your truth, and making sure your actions match your words. It's about choosing relationships, romantic, platonic, professional, where people don't just say the right things, but actually do the right things.

You've done the work. You've reflected, journaled, grounded your energy, and learned to communicate with clarity and confidence. And if you slip, that's okay. You can always revisit your journal, reread the chapter, or take a breath and begin again.

Growth isn't linear. It's layered.

This journey doesn't have a finish line. There's no magical moment where you suddenly throw your hands up and say, "Aha! I've mastered the *Pearl of Grace*! I'm done now." Growth doesn't work like that. There's no single finish line, just an ever-evolving path of self-discovery, self-worth, and self-expression. Every phase of life brings new lessons, deeper clarity, and a greater understanding of your own voice. Every challenge is an opportunity to strengthen your confidence, expand your wisdom, and refine how you connect with the world around you.

And through it all, GRACE is your guide. Grace is that quiet, unwavering inner knowing. It's the strength that whispers, "You are worthy. You are capable. You don't need permission to take up space." Grace is the energy of divine support, whether you call it God, the Universe, Spirit, or simply your highest self. Grace also shows up in the people who uplift you, who remind you of your power when you've forgotten, who nudge you forward when your path feels uncertain.

For introverted, shy, or quiet women, this journey is especially sacred. It's easy to shrink back. It's easy to let others talk over you, to avoid confrontation, or to believe that your voice doesn't matter as much as someone else's. But that's a lie you no longer need to carry. You have a PEARL inside you, a message, a truth, a wisdom that is uniquely yours and meant to be shared. The world needs your voice, not the perfect version, but the *real* one.

Keep walking this path, one step, one word, one truth at a time.

The *Pearl of Grace* isn't just a theory. It's a lived, breathing practice. It's the daily choice to show up with intention, speak your truth with clarity, and ensure that your communication reflects who you really are. It's not about perfection. It's about presence. Grace isn't just soft and gentle. It's strong, bold, and unwavering. And so are you.

The *Pearl of Grace* in action is about choosing yourself. It's about embracing your inner wisdom, honoring your voice, and standing firmly in your worth, especially when it's uncomfortable, especially when it would be easier to stay silent. It's choosing to take up space, to be seen, to be heard, and to be respected.

Your journey isn't over, it's just evolving. There are new levels of confidence, clarity, and connection waiting for you. Each conversation, each boundary, each moment of self-reflection is an invitation to rise even further into your power. As you continue to walk this path, never forget: you are seen, you are heard, you are worthy.

And your voice, it matters more than you know.

You've done the deep work. You've reflected, grounded, rewired, reclaimed, and reignited your voice. You've walked the *Pearl of Grace,* and now it's time to live it out loud. Say what you mean. Set the boundary. Ask the question. Take up the space. Not because you've "become someone else", but because you've finally come home to yourself.

You are not too much. You are not too quiet. You are not invisible. You are a force of clarity, courage, and connection.

Let grace lead you. Let it ground you in the hard conversations, carry you through the wobbly moments, and remind you that strength and softness can exist together. Grace isn't just what you offer others. It's what you return to within yourself.

So go out there. Speak boldly. Love deeply. Live unapologetically. Shine with intention, with presence, and with power. Go shine your pearl, with grace.

And if you ever forget, flip back a page. Take a breath. Open your journal. Reconnect to your grace.

You've got this. Because the truth is, you *always* have.

Dear Worthy One,

You have walked this journey with me, step by step, word by word, breath by breath. And for that, I thank you from the depths of my heart.

This book was never just about learning communication skills. It was about remembering the power that has always been within you. The wisdom, the truth, the courage to speak, create, and express yourself fully. You have taken the time to explore, reflect, and reconnect with your voice, and that is something to celebrate.

Know this: **Your voice *matters*. Your truth *matters*.** The world needs your presence, your wisdom, and the way only you can share it. Whether you are still finding your way or already stepping into your power, trust that your journey is unfolding exactly as it should.

I hope this book has given you not just good insights, but a renewed sense of confidence, grace, and empowerment to share your voice with clarity and authenticity. And if you ever doubt yourself, come back to these pages and to the knowing that you are meant to be heard.

Thank you for allowing me to be part of your life´s special journey. May you continue to shine, speak, and embrace the beautiful truth of who you are.

With gratitude and grace,
Grace C.W. Liu
The Woman's Truth Awakener & Professional Communication Strategist

Your Call-to-Action: Embrace Your Pearl of Grace™

Congratulations, Beautiful Soul, for making it this far. You've taken the courageous step to dive deep into discovering the *Pearl of Grace* within you. Through these pages, you've learned the power of your voice, the wisdom of silence, and the art of speaking with confidence, clarity, and grace.

This journey is about reclaiming your worth, stepping into your truth, and embracing who you are, at your very core. It is about empowering yourself to be seen, heard, and understood without fear, without anxiety, and without over-explaining. By now, you understand that your unique voice is your greatest asset, and the world is waiting for you to share it.

As you move forward, remember that this transformation does not end with the last page here. *Pearl of Grace* is a *lifelong journey* of self-discovery and communication mastery. Now that you have unlocked the wisdom within, it is time to carry it with you into your interactions and conversations, your relationships, and your everyday life.

Your Next Steps

Deepen Your Practice
Use the ***Grace in Action Workbook*** to continue your journey through the *Pearl of Grace* framework. Inside, you'll find reflective journal prompts, practical tools, and guided exercises that help you integrate both the PEARL and GRACE principles into your everyday life. It's your next step toward living and communicating with clarity, confidence, and compassion.

Amplify Your Voice with the *YOU MATTER, Yes You Do!* Card Deck
These reflective prompts are designed to help you recognize your worth, speak your truth, and shift from anxious to empowered—one card at a time.

Lighten Your Load with the *Liu (Loo) Loo Life's Wisdom In Every Flush* Deck
Sometimes you need to flush the funk. This fun, sassy deck helps you shake off heavy energy and approach life (and communication) with humor, heart, and wisdom.

Discover Your Communication Style
Start with the free Know Your Unique Communication Style quiz to understand how you naturally express yourself—and how to lean into your strengths while growing your confidence. Take the quiz: https://gracesoulutions.com/quiz.

Dare to Ask for More—With Grace, Not Guilt: *10 Tips to Ask for What You Want—Without Guilt, Fear, or Overthinking (Free Guide)*

If you've ever struggled to ask for what you truly want without guilt, fear, or overthinking, this free guide is your next gentle nudge. Inside, you'll find 10 soulful and practical tips to help you start asking with confidence, courage, and calm.

Download it here: https://gracesoulutions.com/daretoask

Explore the Grace Notes Card Deck Collection

From soulful reflection to real talk in relationships, from workplace expression to generational wisdom and teen empowerment, each volume of Grace Notes supports a different facet of your communication journey:

- **Grace Notes Vol. 1** - Soulful Reflection
- **Grace Notes Vol. 2** - Real Talk Relationships
- **Grace Notes Vol. 3** - Speak Up at Work
- **Grace Notes Vol. 4** - Legacy Messages
- **Grace Notes Vol. 5** - Teen Spark

Whether you pull a card daily or use them alongside this book, Grace Notes help you return to your voice with intention and grace.

Ready for More Support? Explore the Gracefully Unmuted Masterclass
–Gracefully Unmuted: Go From Quiet to Confident—Speak Up, Ask Boldly, and Be Heard

This upcoming masterclass is being thoughtfully designed for shy, quiet, and covertly unspoken women who feel like they can't ask for what they truly want or need—at work, in relationships, or even with themselves.

You'll be guided to release communication blocks, shift from self-doubt to vocal power, and begin speaking up with confidence and grace—without overexplaining or feeling like you're "too much."

When the masterclass opens, you'll discover:

- Practical tools to express yourself clearly and calmly
- Mindset shifts to stop second-guessing your worth
- Soulful encouragement and empowering guidance

Because your voice matters—and it's time to be seen, heard, and understood.

To be the first to know when registration opens, download the free guide:

10 Tips to Ask for What You Want—Without Guilt, Fear, or Overthinking: www.GraceSOULutions.com/daretoask

To stay connected and explore additional resources:
 www.GraceSOULutions.com

Stay Connected
I would love to support you as you continue to embrace your *Pearl of Grace*. Here is how we can stay connected:

Follow me on social media for insights, tips, and updates:
Facebook: https://www.facebook.com/GraceChrysalis
Instagram: https://www.instagram.com/gracesoulutions
LinkedIn: https://www.linkedin.com/in/grace-cw-liu
YouTube: https://www.youtube.com/@GraceSOULutions-dy3yq

Have questions or want to connect personally?

Visit GraceSOULutions.com and use the contact form to reach me directly.

Want to go deeper?

Book a consultation here: https://gracesoulutions.com/schedule.

Resources

Human Design
- Free Chart Options:

Jovian Archive – https://www.jovianarchive.com/get_your_chart

My Human Design – https://www.myhumandesign.com/

Enneagram
- Free Test Options:

Truity – https://www.truity.com/test/enneagram-personality-test

Enneagram Universe – https://enneagramuniverse.com/enneagram/test/complete-enneagram-test

For a full summary of Enneagram communication styles and journaling prompts, refer to the Companion Workbook.

Pearl of Grace Collection by Grace C.W. Liu

A curated collection of card decks and a companion workbook are designed to support your journey through the *Pearl of Grace.* These tools stand alone or can be used together to help you embody soulful communication, confidence, and emotional resilience.

Grace in Action Workbook
A practical companion to the *Pearl of Grace* book. Includes journal prompts, mindset tools, and reflection exercises to help you integrate the PEARL and GRACE frameworks into your daily life.

Grace Notes Volume 1: Soulful Reflection
Speak your truth. Own your worth. Let grace guide your growth.

A 63-card deck offering daily doses of truth, healing, and inspired communication. Each card includes a soul statement and a Pearl Practice to guide your voice with clarity and heart.

Grace Notes Volume 2: Real Talk Relationships
Get real. Stay grounded. Heal with honesty.
A 40-card deck for navigating communication in close relationships. Speak your needs, set boundaries, and reconnect with care and clarity.

Grace Notes Volume 3: Speak Up at Work
Communicate like a leader—with soul, strategy, and strength.
A 40-card deck to help you express yourself in professional settings. From asking for a raise to navigating workplace dynamics, these cards bring emotional intelligence into your career.

Grace Notes Volume 4: Legacy Messages
Your voice is your legacy. Let it echo with grace.
A 40-card deck for women ready to pass down wisdom, navigate generational conversations, and speak the truths that matter most with intention and heart.

Grace Notes Volume 5: Teen Spark
Your voice matters. Let it shine with sass, soul, and self-respect.
A 40-card deck created for teen girls (ages 12–18) to help them speak up, trust themselves, and navigate challenges with confidence and clarity.

Other Card Decks by Grace C.W. Liu

YOU MATTER, Yes You Do! Card Deck
A 62-card journal prompt deck designed to help you reflect on your worth, shift your mindset, and reconnect with what matters most. Use

it for self-care moments or in daily journaling to remind yourself—you matter.

- U.S. Residents (Physical Deck):
  https://gracesoulutions.com/you-matter-yes-you-do-card-deck-and-journal

- Digital Version (Worldwide): Available on Deckible –
  https://www.deckible.com/card-decks/4tU-you-matter-yes-you-do-embody-your-worthiness-unlock-your-voice-say-goodbye-to-anxiety-speak-with-confidence-grace-c-w-liu

Liu (Loo) Loo Life's Wisdom In Every Flush Card Deck
A sassy, playful deck that delivers bite-sized life wisdom—one flush at a time. Featuring quirky cat art and fun prompts, this 56-card deck helps you release the messy stuff and laugh through life's crap storms.

- U.S. Residents (Physical Deck):
  https://gracesoulutions.com/product/liu-loo-loo-lifes-wisdom-in-every-flush

- Digital Version (Worldwide): Available on Deckible –
  https://www.deckible.com/card-decks/4w0-liu-loo-loo-life-s-wisdom-in-every-flush-let-wisdom-flow-with-every-flush-of-life-s-lessons-grace-c-w-liu

U.S. residents may purchase the physical decks using the links above or access digital versions through the Deckible app.

Journaling

Josette Diaz, Self Awareness Coach for Midlife Women
Self-awareness mentor guiding deeper reflection and clarity through creative strategies.

Connect: http://Guidancetowellness.com or Instagram: @josettediaz

Breathwork

Christina Sommers, a trauma-informed coach integrating finances, breathwork, and nervous system regulation.
Breathwork practitioner helping you release blocks and regulate emotional energy.
Connect:
https://breathofrenewal.com or email: hello@breathofrenewal.com

Card Deck Creation

Rosie Battista, Creative Consultant & Card Deck Publisher, aka Queen of Card Decks
Want to create your own branded transformational card deck? Learn about Rosie's Creative Services
Connect: https://www.rosiebattista.com or
Follow for Card Deck Delivery Ideas & Insights on
https://www.youtube.com/rosiebattista

Quantum Level Reprogramming

Arica Vaughn, Master Practitioner and Teacher of Quantum Level Reprogramming support for transformative subconscious reprogramming to heal wounds and expand self-worth.
Connect:
https://www.aricavaughn.com or
Email: connect@aricavaughn.com.

Underground Radio C

Cari Hansen, Owner Founder. Radio/TV Host Producer and Podcaster
Radio host of Underground Radio C, offering empowering conversations that inspire women to find and amplify their voice by listening to powerful stories and interviews.
Connect:
Facebook:
https://www.facebook.com/UndergroundRadioC?mibextid=wwXIfr&mibextid=wwXIfr
YouTube: https://youtube.com/@undergroundradioc7300

Listen to Grace's featured episode:
https://www.youtube.com/live/Dzi2PJwmxIo?feature=shared

Joy in the Conversation

Lynn Whitbeck, CEO & Founder Petite2Queen
Sales strategist helping women create joyful and confident sales conversations.
Connect:
Schedule a Joyful Sales Conversation:
https://calendly.com/p2q/joyful-convo-session

Download the free guide - *Joyful Sales: 3 Steps to Quickly Grow Your Business*: https://get.petite2queen.com/joyfulsalesblueprint

Financial Empowerment

Lea Tran, Wealth Protection Strategist. Foreword Contributor for
Pearl of Grace
Empowers women, families, and entrepreneurs to safeguard their income and future through living benefits and tax-free retirement planning.

Connect: http://www.LeaTran.com or email: Lea@LeaTran.com

Pearl of Grace Self-Care Kit

Laura Kinnaman-Spears, Skincare Consultant
Creator of the Pearl of Grace Self-Care Kit, featuring Mary Kay products for soul-nurturing self-care inspired by Grace's personal rituals.
Connect: http://www.marykay.com/lkinnaman-spears or
Instagram: @laurakinnamanspears

Acknowledgements

Disclaimer:
Some names and identifying details have been changed in this book to protect the privacy of individuals. The scenarios shared are based on personal experiences, client stories, or common situations used to illustrate key lessons. Any resemblance to actual persons, living or dead, is purely coincidental.

Mentors & Communities

To my past and present mentors—both in life and in business—and to the incredible friends and networking communities who've walked alongside me—including 262 Women, Her Nation Club, Alignable, eWomen Network, and She Rises Studios—thank you for your guidance, inspiration, and belief in me. Whether for a season or a lifetime, your support left a lasting imprint. I've learned firsthand that surrounding yourself with the right people truly matters. This book exists because of the powerful community I chose to grow with.

Professional Support Team

To my past and present mindset coaches, thank you for expanding my inner landscape and helping me shift old stories into new possibilities. Your insight and encouragement strengthened the voice behind every page of this book.

To Pullman Marketing, your partnership in bringing my vision to life from designing my website to supporting my early steps in business is something I will always be deeply grateful for.

To Rosie Battista, thank you for inspiring the design direction of this book cover. Your creative spirit helped shape the visual heart of this project in a way that feels both soulful and aligned.

To Sally Lotz, my book coach, and to Katelyn Silva and her team—thank you for helping to refine this manuscript with clarity, precision, and grace. Your thoughtful edits and encouragement made this book even more powerful.

Media & Creative Collaborators

To Deb Drummond and the women of the 262 Women community, thank you for your continued support, collaboration, and inspiration.

To Cari Hansen, thank you for the opportunity to be a guest on Underground Radio C and for the space you hold to amplify women's voices.

To the incredible women who generously said "Yes!" to being featured or listed as additional resources in this book, thank you for sharing your expertise, wisdom, and heart. Your presence adds even more depth and value for the readers on this journey.

Friends & Family

To my personal friends—there are too many of you to name without turning this into another chapter. Thank you for cheering me on, lifting me up, and adding your sparkle to this journey. Your support, laughter, and creative energy meant more than you know.

To my husband and my parents, thank you for believing in me and standing by my side through the highs, the lows, and the late-night writing sessions. Your love and encouragement mean more than words can ever express.

To the courageous women I've coached, walked alongside, or learned from—Your willingness to show up, share vulnerably, and rise into your truth has deeply inspired the heart of this book. Whether it was through a conversation, a story, or a breakthrough moment, your journeys helped shape the pages within. A special thanks to those who allowed me to share your stories as guiding lights for others—your voice matters, and I'm honored to witness your growth.

And to myself—For trusting the message, the mission, and the messy middle. For honoring the whispers of grace, even when the way wasn't clear. For showing up, writing through doubt, and speaking even when silence felt safer. This book is a love letter to others, yes—but also to the part of me that finally chose to be seen and heard.

Spiritual Acknowledgment

To the Divine, thank you for the whispers, the timing, and the grace that guided this journey. The alignment of my name, my message, and my mission has never been more clear. I am deeply grateful.

This book exists because of all of you. Thank you for being part of this journey with me.

Thank You

Thank you so much for reading *Pearl of Grace*! Especially if you enjoyed it, would you leave your honest review on the book page? It truly helps reach other readers and encourages them to check it out.